BOOM!

THERE GOES
YOUR RESOLVE

**A Guide to Ultimate Success in Real Estate
for Realtors and Homeowners Alike**

AL N. FILIPPONE

To my dad, Louis F. Filippone, a World War II veteran and war hero who received numerous medals during his service in the Philippines and who wrote about his time there, and from whom I inherited my interest in writing.

CONTENTS

INTRODUCTION

*"When scripted in Chinese, the word 'crisis' is
written in two characters—one represents danger,
and the other represents opportunity."*
—John F. Kennedy

When I was in my first training class, about to launch my real estate career, the instructor informed us that we were going to have a special guest the next day. That special guest turned out to be Bill Raveis, the owner of the firm I had recently affiliated myself with. Raveis was regarded as a real estate maverick even then, in 1987, and I still remember the question he asked us that day: What do you think will be your biggest challenge in your real estate career? Half the class raised their hands to answer, but no one, including me, offered what Bill wanted to hear. As we exhausted our responses, Bill finally enlightened us. "It will be maintaining your resolve," he matter-of-factly explained.

Thirty-five years later, as the founder and team leader of Connecticut's most successful real estate team and the "Coaching Czar" for the William Raveis Team Development Program, I've learned over and over that resolve—or, rather, the lack of it—is the crux of the reason 87% of realtors fail within five years of entering the business.

In real estate, knowing what to do is not the challenge; that part is simple. What's tough is mustering the commitment to do those things consistently, day in and day out, even when the results aren't immediately there. Creativity is all well and good, but as long as you follow the blueprint and remain committed and focused, the basics can get you there just as easily. My goal with this book, and with all of my advice, is to inspire new and experienced agents alike and make it clear that growing a successful real estate business takes time. As in all fields, the seemingly instant successes and overnight sensations have been in existence for a lot longer than you might think. Case in point: Starbucks was founded In 1971 and Ralph Lauren in 1969. The founders had one thing in common, something required of all of us who have lofty goals: They put their head down and carried on with their dreams.

As my own business evolved, I realized there was a parallel between real estate and life itself. I found that parallel not only interesting but amusing, which is why I began to share my experiences in a blog entitled The Daily Tonic. I've used many of those musings as the basis for this book—and taken them quite a bit further, as well as updated them for today's real estate market.

Along with offering life lessons anyone can use, I've included tips for current and future homeowners alike, as well as advice for those who want to make real estate their career. Because no matter how crazy the market (or the world) gets, there are certain truths that will beyond a doubt lead to success—and fulfillment.

CHAPTER 1

RIDING THE WAVES OF ADVERSITY

When I entered the real estate business in 1987, I knew right away that there were some clear choices before me. I was 32 years old and had just left the field of education. I'd always been sort of an introvert, and I wondered if being successful in real estate meant abandoning my true self and becoming a more outgoing, "pushy" salesperson. Besides that, I wondered if I could really become a success with no business experience whatsoever. Would I join the crowd at the watercooler, where agents engaged in gossip about town politics, office politics and everything in between? Or would I emulate the ones who were at their desk, head down, making calls and focused solely on real estate?

The answer became evident quite quickly. I was single with no children, and I needed to feed and clothe myself. The agents who were most focused were the ones closing the most deals. And while many people view real estate brokers as aggressive, I realized early on that being thorough, staying on top of things and putting in a full week's work (along with weekend appointments) was far more important than strong-arming anyone. As for my lack of experience, I was about to learn what I needed to know by observing others.

Yet as my business grew, I found myself wanting more. I envied the few agents who seemed to have a hold on the high end of the market while doubting I could attain that kind of success myself. One thing I was beginning to realize was that real estate, like life itself, has a rhythm of its own, often moving at a breakneck pace with multiple twists and turns in each transaction. It's easy to get discouraged on behalf of your clients who can't find the home they are looking for. It's also understandable to feel the frustration of sellers who are having a challenge finding a buyer willing to pay their asking price. And those feelings of discouragement or frustration only become magnified if, once a match is made, an unfavorable building inspection or some other event makes it necessary to begin again.

But these kinds of setbacks are not necessarily a bad thing. Indeed, to me, that up-and-down rhythm is part of the beauty of the business, and the beauty of life. Recently, I read about a college athlete who suffered a severe injury—one that would prevent him from finishing out the season and possibly affect his chances of signing a professional contract and earning millions of dollars. Yet the young man was seemingly nonplussed. In his mind, there was no question that going through the process of recovering was going to make him stronger and a better player.

That kind of optimism and focus drives success, whatever goal you're pursuing. Circumstances change from day to day, hour to hour, even minute to minute, as is evidenced by our 24/7 news cycle and social media. For some of us, this rhythm of change can be a great elixir, one that gives us the resolve to move forward. If you can find an opportunity in new and unexpected challenges, you are sure to excel. As

Emerson wrote, "This time, like all times, is a very good one, if we but know what to do with it."

Being able to roll with life's ups and downs also means acquainting yourself with failure. It sounds counterintuitive, but failure is the nature of business—every business meets adversity at one time or another. Any business owner who refuses to acknowledge this is creating unrealistic expectations and setting themselves up for failure. Businesses that thrive become stronger in the face of misfortune. Hotel magnate Bill Marriott once commented, "An opportunist is one who finds the wolf at the front door and appears the next day wearing a fur coat."

Thinking about the upside of (supposed) misfortunes brings to mind an experience I had when my son was in high school playing on his freshman basketball team. Between games, I stepped out into the hallway to take a break when I heard loud bursts of repeated applause. Reentering the gymnasium, I realized there was a half-time exhibition taking place; the players were disabled high schoolers. Afterward, I couldn't stop thinking about those kids and reflecting on why they had made such an impression of me. I understood that it was because they had no concerns about missed shots, mishandling the ball or embarrassing themselves in front of the crowd. These kids simply played with pure, unadulterated passion and heart. They could easily have focused on any number of reasons to not participate, but instead, they put their whole selves into the game. If all of us could only exhibit that kind of freedom and courage, we would get so much more satisfaction out of our relationships, career and life.

I still remember one gorgeous afternoon when I got away from work for a couple of hours to play golf with my two boys. At the time, my youngest son was 13, and he turned out to be the educator that day. We were on the fourth hole and his tee shot landed behind a scattering of trees. For his second shot, he was aiming to hit the ball between two towering elms. I cautioned him that he didn't have a whole lot to gain by doing so and that it would be much safer to just pitch out to the left of them. If he was successful with his strategy, he would be closer to the hole for his next shot, but in my mind, and because of his inexperience, the risk wasn't worth the reward.

Luckily for him, he disagreed, as he did with just about everything I said in those days, and attempted the tricky shot. He hit the ball flush, cleared the trees and set himself up beautifully for his approach to the green. "There you go, Dad," he beamed. "You've got to have confidence!"

I smiled back. Sometimes it's more than that, I thought. Sometimes, you've got to have ignorance. My son didn't have years of experience hitting trees, as I did. Like those kids on the basketball court, he also didn't have a fear of failure. What he did have was naivete, passion and hope.

The bottom line: Embrace adversity and change. Both can reveal your weaknesses, but if you're truly determined to succeed, you'll be inspired to throw your authentic self into all things worthwhile and turn those weaknesses into strengths.

CHAPTER 2

PASSION AND AUTHENTICITY ARE THE KEY TO SATISFACTION—AND SUCCESS

"Authenticity is your greatest asset. Lose your authenticity and you've lost everything."
—Marcus Buckingham

I had dinner with a friend the other day, and something she said stuck in my mind as essential wisdom, both for life and for success as a realtor. "All one needs to do to find true happiness is to remain authentic," she mused. To me, that's the core of what it takes to become a top realtor.

The most memorable relationships I've had at the workplace, whether with clients or colleagues, always turn out to be the most authentic. But it's not always easy to be your true self—or even to know your true self. One of the most challenging areas for realtors, especially those who are relatively new to the business, is discovering their "voice" in a very crowded marketplace. When I use the word "voice," I mean taking actions that coincide with who you are as an individual—being genuine. If you try to be someone other than who you are, the tasks before you will seem even more daunting and, at best, make you squirm with discomfort (unless you have a total lack of genuineness). As I alluded to earlier, at the beginning of my career, I wondered if making a living selling real estate was going to require being a "pushy" salesperson. I had no idea what to expect. Except for selling booster tickets in Little League in fifth, sixth and seventh grade, I had zero sales experience. "If experience is what it takes to succeed," I thought, "my prospects for success will be dismal." I am many things, but a disingenuous fast-talker is not part of the fabric of who I am.

I learned quickly that there was no need to be an aggressive salesperson if I tapped into two of my core strengths: thoroughness and consistency. I had my daily routines and I stuck to them. Every morning at 8:00 A.M. I called homeowners whose homes failed to sell to learn if they were interested in changing realtors. I followed up daily with people I met at open houses, with past clients, with current clients and with my social network, executing my direct-mail and door-knocking strategies. That consistency put me at the "head of the class"—slickness of tongue was not required.

It was a relief to find I could maintain my authenticity and still provide the knowledge, service and expertise that clients expected. Furthermore, I learned that being genuine not only brings success but also increases one's self-esteem and contentment in life. I learned that giving my clients my best advice, whether preparing their home for sale, pricing it, figuring out the best timing, or any of the nuances involved when purchasing a home served me well every time, even when that advice was not in my best interest. I gave the same advice in real estate matters as I would to my family, and it always worked out well and inspired a great sense of satisfaction in me.

In business—or any relationship, for that matter—it's tough to maintain happiness if you lose you. Or, in the words of marketing and strategy expert Stephen Burnett: "Do your work with your whole heart, and you will succeed—there is so little competition."

CHAPTER 3

DETERMINATION, RESOLVE AND COMMITMENT PAY OFF

I t was late December 1987, my very first year in the business. I was the only agent in the office when the aforementioned company founder Bill Raveis saw me as he was leaving. We briefly chatted, and he reflected back on a time when he was a single agent like me, working with just a few others in his office. It was Christmas Eve and he got a call to show a home. It was fortuitous that he was there, because the potential buyer was the head of a large relocation enterprise; by just showing up, Bill got an exclusive deal that ended up being a game changer for the company. I always think of this when things speed up just as I'm preparing to take some time off. The agents that get to the office when others don't end up reaping the benefits.

I once received a call on one of my listings the day before Christmas. Truthfully, I didn't really feel like showing the house, but I went ahead and met the client at the property. He was quite enthralled with the offering and asked if he could return to see the home with his partner later that afternoon. I obliged, and, two days later, they made a full-price offer that was accepted. After that, I never made the mistake of thinking any particular day or time of year, whether the winter holidays or the height of summer vacation, would be void of activity.

Of course, there are patterns to real estate. It tends to run in cycles of 90 days or more, meaning your business load in the fall is generally predicated on the prospecting you did in the summer, a time many of us want to slow down and relax—or, at least, when we assume everyone is out of town. The same goes for the holidays. Yet these supposedly "dead" times are exactly when just showing up can reap tremendous rewards.

I've seen it time and time again when watching professional sports, particularly when teams are evenly matched. It's often the will to win that makes the difference. The same is true in real estate. The constant changes in the market can make the business feel like an emotional roller coaster. Add to that the competition, which is stiff and plentiful, and it becomes evident how crucial it is to maintain your commitment to professionalism, to act in the best interest of your clients and maintain resolve at all times.

Commitment to whatever drives you is one of the spices of life. If a venture is not worth a full commitment, then it's not worth engaging in at all. By now, you know I like to quote people, and one of my favorites is this succinct piece of advice suggested by Pythagoras: "Rest satisfied with doing well and leave others to talk of you as they please."

One example of that commitment comes from Regis McKenna, Steve Jobs's first marketing consultant at Apple. McKenna understood that half-hearted commitments are destined to lead to a state of frustration and leave you feeling unfulfilled. Maybe that's why, on his business cards, it read: "Regis McKenna – Himself." No fancy title, because McKenna's message was simple: Of all his responsibilities, his greatest responsibility to the world was to be himself. Far from egocentric, he recognized that to make a meaningful contribution to anything—whether a relationship, a group, an organization or, yes, to oneself, you have to make a full commitment.

Of course, ego can, and often does, interfere with decisions, impeding us from considering all options and making choices that are in our best interests. The trouble is, making decisions that are devoid of ego can be challenging, particularly for independent business owners whose decisions can mean the difference between a firm that grows and one that goes bust. That's why it's important to watch for the signs of an unhealthy ego, including the following beliefs:

- I am what I have.
- I am what I do for a living.
- I am what others say about me.
- I am separate from everyone else.

It's much easier to make prudent decisions with confidence if you are able separate the pros and cons from insecurities that emanate from a delicate ego.

So the next time you're facing a decision, whether about prioritizing time, money or other common issues, check your ego. It will be easier to trust your instincts, choose with peace of mind and fully commit. For many of us, it is difficult to make full commitments to what we do. Often, it seems as if we're running away from fear. But wouldn't it be better if we ran straight toward our dreams?

Periodically, I ask myself, "How many things do people fully commit to in their world?" It's a question I recommend asking yourself. If the answer feels unsatisfying, it's time to reflect further. Are you not fully committing because of poor time management or lack of motivation? Do you become anxious at the thought of fully committing to anything?

I've come to the conclusion that getting past fear is about finding what inspires you. That idea crystallized for me a few years back when I got involved with Vinyasa Yoga. It was something I'd been considering for a while, but I had some trepidation because the class took place in a studio where the temperature was set at 100 degrees. Daunting, to say the least. But I was determined to forge ahead. I was getting older and was passionate about staying healthy. Though I was eating well, I decided I needed more. I remember the first class as if it were yesterday. I was exhausted and perspiring profusely, thinking it would never end. Once it did, I recall a lightheadedness and a thought running through my mind along the lines of, "This is either going to be the best thing I've ever done for myself or I'm going to die!" I seriously thought that I might, but I didn't. And I proceeded to go nearly every day for two years, understanding that if I stopped, it would be too easy to never go back. My inspiration to be healthy and look good overcame my fear of the unknown.

Operating from a place of abundance is another way to combat fear. So many of us talk about having too much stuff, of wanting to downsize and simplify. I've come to realize that abundance is not necessarily a bad thing. Many see abundance as tantamount to selfishness, but nothing could be further from the truth. The theme of abundance is even sprinkled throughout the Bible, with scriptures alluding to it as something that is offered to those who trust and have faith, not fear.

In real estate, abundance can allow you to better meet your responsibilities as a realtor and to provide your clients with better service. We were placed on earth to enjoy abundance and to share it with others.

Of course, you can't share what you don't have. The most surefire way to create what you need is to grow what you do have. A realtor who lacks business and has just a few clients may be more anxious about losing a client than a realtor who is servicing many. That fear of loss can lead to telling a client what they want to hear rather than what they need to hear—and result in bad advice, leading to poor decisions on your client's part.

It doesn't have to be that way. I recently read a quote that stuck with me: "If you generate, you don't have to tolerate." A realtor with an abundance of business has an opportunity to gain valuable experience. That abundance can place them in a position to resist temptations that are driven by fear. To be able to give their clients their best advice (whether or not the client wants to hear it) without having to worry about consequences or losing the business is a gift, and it only happens because the agent is not "living and dying" over that one deal.

A part of generating abundance is becoming multifaceted, which, in the case of real estate, means having a lot of business to attend to on any given day. But don't confuse multifaceted with multitasking. The latter actually leads to accomplishing less than when you "close your circles"—complete one task before moving on to another.

Being multifaceted creates an abundance of opportunity. To use a real estate example, if half of what you work on closes and you've had 40 bona fide buyer and seller opportunities, then you've had a good year, closing on 20 properties. The drive to create these opportunities emanates from your heart and soul, so it certainly helps if you love your life and the work you do. That choice is yours. You can sit in the corner and suck your thumb, or you can heed Winston Churchill's advice: "A pessimist sees the difficulty in every opportunity; an optimist sees the opportunity in every difficulty."

I find the following questions can inspire the right attitude toward challenges:

- How do you handle adversity?
- What can you do to improve upon that moving forward?
- Is loving your life a choice?

By cultivating an abundance mindset, you can also increase your:

- Security
- Self-esteem
- Confidence
- Business stability
- Number of transactions that close

One thing that has helped me get past fear and pursue abundance was to resolve to spend a year saying yes more often. In general, I'm not a New Year's resolution guy; in my observation, most people seem to quickly forget their resolutions or replace them with others. But back in 2012, instead of resolving to lose weight or earn more money or do a better job keeping in touch with family, I became a "yes man." After all, yes elicits so much more energy than no. And when I reflected back on many of the times I'd said no, I realized my response had been based on fear. We can all benefit from more energy and less fear.

Saying yes can inspire:

- Exploration
- Experimentation
- Freedom
- Creative thinking
- Exuberance
- Confidence
- Trust

How can you accurately assess if you have been living with a "yes" mentality? Below, some tell-tale signs:

- You have more energy than usual.
- Others seem to be more positive when they are around you.
- You are more comfortable in the presence of others who are positive.
- You seem to trust in the universe more than you have in the past.
- You're less apt to try and control those things you know cannot be controlled.
- You have been getting the results you've been striving for more consistently, and those results seem to be accomplished by working smarter, not necessarily harder.

- You're more aligned with your goals (versus being at odds with them).
- You've noticed an increase in your self-esteem.
- You get up in the morning with more enthusiasm for the day ahead.

CHAPTER 4

YOUR SUCCESS
INCLUDES OTHERS

I tend to throw around the word "success" a lot—indeed, it's probably one of the most frequently used words in most books on business. Yet ask 100 people what success means to them and you're likely to get as many different answers. For some, success is associated with income; for others, it might be reaching a certain level in their field. I have a somewhat different perspective. To me, success includes having people's best interests at heart. That means:

- Inspiring and helping team members be the best they can be so they can achieve their goals
- Giving clients the best advice possible—the same advice I would give to a dear friend or relative
- Providing team members with a secure, stable environment and clarity of purpose

- Giving team members the necessary tools to get the order every single time
- Feeling that I'm putting forth my best effort every day

A few years ago, I had a conversation with another real estate broker. Our team was experiencing a meteoric rise, and I must have conveyed that because he felt the need to remind me how much all of us need others. "Everyone needs a mentor of some sort," he said. "Every successful person has someone with whom they consult. We all need support." Not any mentor will do, however. In making your choice, there are a number of things to consider:

- The length and quality of their experience in the field
- Their strengths and weaknesses versus yours. It's best when you can compensate for one another's vulnerabilities.
- Whether your personalities complement one another
- Their business perspective and philosophy on life
- Their commitments outside the realm of their chosen field, whether familial, personal, or otherwise, that will take them away from a commitment that is in balance with yours

I can certainly attest to the wisdom of finding a mentor—and working as a team in general. Even as our own real estate team was growing, there were naysayers aplenty. There were also those who took issue with the team concept entirely, a judgment based, in my opinion, on fear and egos that were a bit large.

The cynics believed that clients would want to work only with the team leader, making other team members superfluous. My goal was to make sure that every team member was outstanding in their own right, including administrative staff, stagers, and everyone who played a role in the operations. We as individuals generally cannot accomplish everything we would like to on our own—it takes support. If you resist this notion, I suggest asking yourself:

- What's stopping me from understanding other people's perspectives?
- What makes some people more open to hearing another person's point of view?
- Is the necessity of guidance and support something I had to learn the hard way?
- Am I getting the support I need to succeed?

I saw that need for support firsthand while playing in a golf tournament with a scratch golfer. It was a match play format, and as we headed down the first fairway, we discussed our strategy. "Whatever you do," he said, "don't leave me hanging." For those of you who don't play golf, he was essentially asking me to keep my ball in play. He didn't want to be solely responsible for winning the hole. "I don't play well under those circumstances," he admitted.

"How interesting," I thought. A player with that kind of talent, and he needed my support in order to maintain the confidence to play at a high level.

I thought of his comment on a gorgeous summer day as I talked with one of the realtors in our office. She was giving me one of many updates on a sale she had been working on, one that had taken more twists and turns than either of us cared to think about. She represented the buyer, and one of the challenges with the transaction was that the listing agent was AWOL. Our agent had been doing the work of two people. Years ago, I learned that some realtors work with you, some work against you and some don't work at all. I suppose the third scenario is better than the second. Yet there is no disputing the exponential difference in the closing rate when realtors partner with one another, including:

- You are less distracted and thus more able to maintain a laser-sharp focus.
- You're less likely to feel overwhelmed.

- You can be more productive.
- You're better able to provide your client with clarity as challenges unfold.
- You're more likely to offer better solutions to challenges.
- Each party to the transaction feels they were better served and is more apt to have a satisfying experience.

In the end, being destructive to one means destruction for all, including yourself. The other choice is to offer unconditional support and allow everyone's star to shine...including yours! In the best cases, becoming part of a team can help you grow. At one point in my career, I realized that even arising at 5:00 A.M., I no longer had enough hours in the day to accomplish all I wanted. If that strikes a chord with you, it might be time to become part of a team—by hiring a personal assistant. In essence, it can help you expand yourself by leveraging the power of another. Yet some people, realtors included, feel overwhelmed by the idea, wondering:

- How do I go about finding someone?
- How do I train them?
- How do I allocate responsibilities?
- What if the work they produce is less than perfect?
- What if I don't have enough work for them?

The answers to the first three questions simply require a bit of planning. Take these steps:

- First, the search: Run an online ad.
- Utilize word of mouth. You'd be surprised by how many people are looking for such work with an eye toward becoming licensed one day.
- Always be on the lookout. Those in the service business, such as excellent restaurant servers, tend to adapt well to other service businesses.

- Nail the job description. Have it prepared before meeting with your candidate(s) for the position.
- Delegate: Hand over any task you detest to a capable person, including those that do not require a license or that are not direct producers of income.

Then comes the question of training. Who has time? The truth is, you've got to carve time out of your day to teach a new hire how things are done. So make an appointment on your calendar to mentor and train. If you don't block out time for training, your hire is destined for failure.

Even then, don't expect perfection. I have found that perfection has a lot to do with ego. When someone claims to be a perfectionist, what they are really saying is that they like to have things done their way and to be in control. To expand yourself, you must be able to relinquish control to others. That's part of being on a team.

Warren Buffet attributes much of his success to delegation. He has said: "Delegate almost to the point of abdication," and has proudly explained that he speaks with the heads of the companies he owns no more than once a year. Delegating allows you to streamline your business and make your strengths the focal point of your day.

Delegating includes giving others permission to make mistakes. Mistake-free environments are paralyzing and stifle growth. The iconic general George S. Patton once said, "Don't tell people how to do things. Tell them what to do and let them surprise you with their results."

I see the benefits of teamwork wherever I look, not just in real estate. In 2011, I watched an interesting interview in the lead-up to the Super Bowl, where the New England Patriots and the New York Giants would be competing for the Lombardi Trophy. The interviewer was discussing the difficulties the Giants had that season. At one point, they had lost four games in a row and things were looking bleak. He was curious as to how the Giants turned things around. The player being interviewed didn't hesitate: "Through it all, we never tried to come up with a scapegoat. No one on the team ever pointed fingers at anyone else." In other words, they remained a true team.

That perspective was in sharp contrast to the one displayed in the playoffs by another NFL team the very next year. The team that eventually lost to the Patriots were immersed in controversy as they prepared for the big game. Essentially, one of the players was less than complimentary about how the team's quarterback had fared the week before, questioning whether he was equipped to play under the pressure of a big game.

To my mind, the fact that the Giants won their game and the aforementioned team lost theirs is no coincidence. When teams are quick to point out the faults of their teammates, the results are seldom positive.

At the risk of overusing football analogies, I have to talk about Super Bowl XLVI, the second time the Giants and the Patriots met on football's biggest stage. The game was one of those contests where it's a shame one team has to lose, but when the final whistle was blown, there was in fact a winner: not only the New York Giants, but Eli Manning, who was named Most Valuable Player.

Like his New England Patriot counterpart, Tom Brady, Eli Manning has a quiet confidence about him. When asked by a radio host at the beginning of the season if he thought he was an elite quarterback, Manning replied, "Yes." Sports reporters were aghast. It was as close as the public had ever gotten to hearing Manning speak glowingly about himself.

Yet Manning has since proven his response to be completely accurate. No one can doubt that he is in fact an elite quarterback. Yet I still remember, after that Super Bowl was over, all Manning wanted to discuss was his teammates—how hard they prepared, how well they played together and the joy everyone took in winning as a team. Manning's confidence is quite different from ego.

Like Manning, I've observed that those who are truly elite in any field seem to have that air of quiet confidence about them. Not cocky, not arrogant, but subtly confident. It's no different in real estate. Many of the realtors who are most accomplished exude a quiet confidence. That's part of what gives clients the feeling of security and trust that is so essential to a successful real estate experience.

Keep in mind that the difference between arrogance and confidence is a fine line. The right kind of confidence comes from the heart, and others can sense it.

CHAPTER 5

JUST LET GO

Recently, I was speaking to a realtor who'd had an opportunity that didn't quite turn out the way she'd hoped, for her or her client. As we chatted, we hypothesized about what she could have done differently. Our conclusion was simple. If given the chance to begin again and chart another course, she would have done everything much the same. "Sometimes I just think the outcome is beyond our control," she concluded. I was impressed because I am older than she is, and it has taken me a lot longer to figure that one out.

As I've seen the ways in which we are all connected, I can't help but believe that much of what goes on in our lives is preordained. That's not to say that we don't have certain responsibilities. We have a responsibility to hone our skills and to work smart; to take whatever fair and prudent steps need to be taken to serve our clients to the best of our abilities. The truth is, we can do all that, and unexpected twists and turns will still come up along the way that are impossible to predict or explain.

That's one reason it's so important not to second-guess yourself. Second-guessing is easy to do in a career as demanding as real estate. But it exponentially adds to one's anxiety level. It's much easier when you realize that much of what happens is beyond your control.

Case in point: I had friends over for dinner one weekend, and before we sat down to eat, there was a request that I make a martini...shaken, not stirred. I had all the necessary ingredients but one significant challenge. I couldn't remove the lid to the martini shaker. Tapping gently on the countertop, tugging, pulling one end while someone else held the other, holding it under hot water—nothing seemed to work, and the more frustrated I felt, the more I began craving a martini myself. So I made one for each of us—stirred. What a disappointment! Why anyone with the choice would order the libation made that way is beyond my comprehension. By the second sip the disappointment was too great. I picked up the shaker and gave it a good whack against the countertop, something I'd been avoiding for fear of denting it. It popped off with nary a nick.

I've seen it written more than once that "fear of loss is a greater motivator than opportunity to gain." I've come to learn that's usually true for most people. During that martini moment, I got to a place where I finally thought, "I don't care if I ruin the darn thing or not; at this point, there's nothing to lose because I can't use it anyway." And the opportunity to gain won out.

That martini made me consider why, in business and in life, when you stop trying to control everything, things just work out. A home lingers on the market forever until the homeowners are resigned and about to remove it from the marketplace. Voilà! Suddenly there are multiple offers. Once you release the tension and negative energy in your mind, your biggest obstacles seem to disappear. By the way, that shaken martini was wonderful!

Letting go isn't the only path to success. Below is a list of truisms—some unique to real estate, others not, that have stood the test of time:

- One size doesn't fit all.
- Be yourself and build on your strengths.
- Don't allow your weaknesses to rent space in your brain.
- Choose to emulate those who focus on growing their business.
- Ignore those who huddle in the corner complaining.
- Know the difference between a "pushy" salesperson and one who is on top of things.
- Communication is critical.
- So, too, is service.
- Consistency is essential.
- So, too, is resolve. (I can't say that often enough.)

It's also important to reflect on the ways you might unknowingly be impeding your growth. I've met many who believe they are predestined to struggle and thus create an imaginary ceiling to their success. It's almost as if they feel guilty about being successful or believe they don't deserve to be and so convince themselves they must make do with the crumbs left by others. When one feels discouraged, it's easy to become emotionally sedentary and immobilized. Inertia, in fact, is probably the most important difference between the movers and shakers of the world and the also-rans. The former remain in motion and realize that doing anything is better than stasis. As leadership guru Soren Kaplan has said, "It doesn't matter what you do next, as long as you do something and learn. The worst thing you can do is sit and stew."

Here are some "obstacles" I've seen colleagues create over the years:

- I don't have children and so I'm deprived of business generated from school and children's social activities.
- I have children and am encumbered with all kinds of responsibilities that impede me from working the hours I need in order to succeed.
- I'm not married and so my social circle is cut in half.

- I'm married and have the additional responsibilities that entails.
- I don't have the resources to belong to a country club and thereby benefit from the connections that affords.
- I don't have the resources to invest in personal promotion.
- My social and business sphere is too young.
- My social and business sphere is too old.

I can probably come up with 20 more such excuses about why success remains elusive. You can likely think of many of your own. The truth of the matter is that none of them are valid. After 35 years in the business, I have seen many individuals with one or more of these issues attain tremendous success.

What obstacles do you formulate in your mind that impede you from creating abundance?

CHAPTER 6

IN THE END, FOR SUCCESSFUL PEOPLE, IT'S ABOUT MUCH MORE THAN THE MONEY

still remember an interview I once saw with the late and great Los Angeles Laker player Kobe Bryant. When asked about his passion and drive to improve his play, he responded that he never considered the time he put into practice as work. To paraphrase the superstar, "I enjoy doing it so much that it wasn't until I was older that I realized it was work."

I can remember having the same thoughts about real estate. I recall one particular Easter Sunday in late April. I was at my grandmother's house, relaxing after one of her patented great Italian meals, when it dawned on me that it was the first day of that year that I wasn't working—including weekends. And I felt good about that. For me, work is fun—a sense of purpose and the thrill of the deal is all I need. Purpose is one of the things that makes a career in real estate so compelling. Yes, it can be stressful at times. Yes, there are moments when you're overcome by a feeling of being unappreciated, or that you're swimming against the tide. But there's nothing like the moment when you close a deal, knowing you are the person who helped someone attain their dream. Every time that happens, I'm reminded that my life has a purpose, and that purpose is to help others.

A few years back, I was driving home from a listing presentation. I remember exactly where I was on the long, sloping road that led to town. The homeowners had just signed a listing contract with me, and I was thinking of the dialogue I'd had with them, the presentation in general and the responsibilities ahead of me. Then I remembered there was a monetary reward that came along with the deal. The financial component, so paramount to so many, was literally the last thing that entered my mind. "Oh, yeah," I thought excitedly. "If the house closes there will be a nice commission check that goes along with it."

It was as if I'd had an awakening. Many of the activities that realtors perform have no compensation attached to them. We do so much for people, and our reward is knowing that we are helping others because we care. How many people can make that claim?

Then there's the thrill of following up on leads, providing potential clients with what they need to make prudent decisions, matching buyers to the near-perfect home for them and procuring the highest price for seller clients. All of that is nothing short of exhilarating.

I have many more responsibilities now than I did that afternoon at my grandmother's house. But what I do still excites me. Over the years, as one executes certain activities many times over, it can become easy to take things for granted, just as we do with the people in our lives. We don't realize how important they are until we lose them.

Once, talking to a colleague about a strategy we were preparing to implement in a specific marketplace, he said something that caught me off guard: "The pursuit of achieving our goal is much more exciting than the monetary rewards attached to it."

My colleague is an excellent businessman, particularly when measured by his ability to generate net profit. But he obviously shares a philosophy of a respected business leader who said, "Success is about thriving, not arriving." I believe success is about both. It certainly is about one's passion to get to the finish line, but it's also about getting to the finish line before anyone else!

Many of us who have attained a goal can look back with fondness on the determination, effort and resolve we put forth in achieving it. There is little doubt we can also remember the feelings of accomplishment that engulfed us when it became clear that we performed a task better than anyone else. (I guess there's a place for ego after all.)

Whatever crazy things are going on in the world, it's important to remember that there is one thing no one can take from us. Work without compensation may not always pay the bills, but it brings rewards that are far greater.

CHAPTER 7

FOLLOW THE 80/20 RULE

We've all heard the saying that the rich get richer. And it's true that 10 to 20 percent of real estate agents conduct 80 to 90 percent of the business. The question is, why?

Some might say that this 80/20 ratio is destiny. The phenomenon was first noted back in 1906 when Italian economist Vilfredo Pareto observed that 20 percent of Italy's residents owned 80 percent of its wealth. He later determined that 20 percent of his crop yielded 80 percent of his produce.

Another thing to understand when considering the Pareto Principle, as it is often referred to, is the power that comes from being the best. In sports, people want to see the best. (It's no secret that TV network executives privately root for the most popular teams or individuals when it comes to competition because they are well aware of the dramatic effect popularity has on their ratings.)

It's no different when it comes to business. People want to work with the best, and so the more business a realtor (or anyone) transacts, the more they are perceived to be the best. Sometimes, success perpetuates itself.

What does that mean for those of us who aren't among the top 20 percent but would like to be? How can you "blossom where you are planted," as the saying goes?

It's also true that 20 percent of one's efforts yield 80 percent of results—and vice versa. So it's not merely a question of working smarter. It's also about working smarter at the right things. That's why you need to determine which 20 percent of your efforts result in the majority of your business.

For me, as I established my career, I focused primarily on direct mail. After reading *The 22 Immutable Laws of Marketing* by Al Reis and Jack Trout, I came away with an understanding of niche marketing and the impact of "narrowing the battlefield." And so I did, every month, year in and year out, doing direct mail to an enclave of 2,500 homes. Eventually, I became known as the specialist in that area and dominated the marketplace with a 30% market share—all from direct mail.

Hone your skills consistently, then engage those skills within the scope of that 20 percent and you will be among the rich getting richer.

THE DOS AND DON'TS OF CHOOSING A REAL-ESTATE AGENT

Deciding who to list with has never been as complicated as it is today, and the explosion of marketing opportunities since the advent of the internet is only part of the reason. This list of bottom-line dos and don'ts offers a good beginning.

- DO choose a realtor with a proven track record of a high sale price/list price ratio. (Translation: someone who is good at pricing and negotiating.)

- DO go with a realtor with a high percentage of listings that actually close, meaning over 90%. (Translation: a good closer who knows how to get the deal done.)
- DO choose a realtor who manages the showings for your home and provides you with detailed feedback for each one. (Translation: someone who puts your interests first so you can make prudent choices moving forward if the home doesn't sell quickly.)
- DO opt for a realtor who practices full-time. (Translation: someone who Is available when a buyer is ready to make a move.)
- DO choose a realtor who provides staging, preferably in-house. (Translation: Staged homes sell more quickly and for more money.)
- DO pick a realtor with a significant web and social media presence. (No translation necessary here.)
- DON'T choose a realtor in the family. Listing your home should never be about nepotism. A friend or relative should be your choice only if you truly believe they are best suited for the job. This is serious business, and while your home may sell immediately, the odds are greater that it won't. There are times during the listing period when you and your realtor will need to have candid discussions. Ask yourself if the relationship you have with them could sustain such frank dialogue. If not, they're not the right choice.
- DON'T forgo staging your home.
- DON'T go with a realtor simply because they offer the lowest commission. A company can't cut fees without cutting services. If a realtor is compromising their commission, their services will also be compromised. Ask yourself: If you're getting estimates for repair work to your home, do you always hire the person who gives you the lowest bid? Or do you hire the one whose work is the best quality? I've seen many people who wear

high-end suits and drive European sports cars hire a discount broker to sell one of their largest investments, essentially creating double jeopardy for themselves. The agent who doesn't charge a full commission is generally less competent. Lack of competence often leads to incorrect pricing, which impedes the sale.

- DON'T make it difficult to show your home. A potential buyer who isn't allowed to view your home on Tuesday is often the person who ultimately purchases another home on Wednesday. Call it the law of intentions or whatever you wish, this occurs much more often than most people realize. Make the procedure for showing your home as convenient for the buyers as possible.

- DON'T make the mistake of thinking that the value you were told when you refinanced is what a real buyer would pay for your home today. The reason: If a lender wants to lend you money, they may estimate a slightly inflated value for your home to justify their equity position. The appraiser may also ignore foreclosure or distress sales to substantiate a higher value. Real buyers in the real world will not.

- DON'T hang around during showings, thinking you can help convince potential buyers. The most beneficial thing you can do is to get as far away as possible. Buying a home is an emotional decision. Buyers like to "try on" a home to see if it feels comfortable to them, and it's awkward to do that when the homeowner is present. In fact, if you're present, buyers may feel they're intruding on your private space. Another benefit of making yourself scarce: The buyer can't ask questions or generate a discussion that isn't in your best interests.

- DON'T resist adjusting the price when the market demands it. The market will determine the price, and your home will sell for what someone is willing to pay for it. If your home doesn't sell within the first 30 days at most, my advice is to do the following:

o If you have frequent showings but no offers, make a 5% adjustment.

o If you have very few showings, make a 10% adjustment.

Other factors to consider and ask for:

- Take testimonials with a grain of salt. While past performance can be a good indicator of how someone will perform for you, I have learned via the hiring process that it's not that difficult to find people who will say good things about anyone. Rather, request that each agent provide you with information that shows their track record with getting their listings sold; the sale price/list price ratio of the properties they sell; median market time; and the market presence of their office.

- Go with a pro. Note their professionalism, including appearance, the questions they ask you and their responses to your questions.

- Look for rapport. A good connection is key, just as it is for anyone you would hire.

- Demand the data. You should have enough data to get a clear view of market conditions and to show there is support for their suggested value of your home. As alluded to earlier, ask the agent to provide the average sale price/list price ratio with homes they have listed.

- Creativity counts. How creative is the strategy they plan to implement to attract buyers to your home? Are they passively waiting for buyers to come or are they aggressively pursuing them via the internet, direct mail and boots-on-the-ground prospecting to find a buyer who loves your home?

- Scope out their scope. Hyper-local experience is not enough. The realtor who can tap into different markets will bring you more buyer activity.

CHAPTER 8

OWNING YOUR FAILURES LEADS TO SUCCESS

Recently, I received my weekly roundup from influencers on LinkedIn, including one from entertainment tycoon Peter Guber: "I have failed over and over and over again in my life," he wrote. "And that is why I succeed."

We all have failures, and it's easy to experience ambivalence and insecurity once you've convinced yourself that you've failed. The conventional wisdom among some business leaders and coaches is that accepting failure leads to more of the same, along with a healthy dose of self-blame, innuendo and excuses.

But what if you could learn to treat failure as your friend? The only way not to fail is to not try—in the case of real estate, to not prospect or generate any business at all. That's what I recently told two realtors who described the letdown they felt when they hadn't been able to turn certain prospects into clients. Disappointment is a good thing. It means you're trying. It can also provide a great opportunity to learn what not to do. As I explained to one of the agents, punishing yourself with thoughts about what you could have done differently—the call you could have made, the person you should have met with—is counterproductive and won't prevent you from missteps in the future.

A few years back, I decided to take my own advice and treat disappointment as a friend. What I mean is taking ownership of it, calmly and rationally. It's not always easy to accomplish, but it's necessary in order to gain a clearer perspective on what to do moving forward, with confidence.

The best way to turn disappointment or failure into opportunity is by doing the following:

- Determine that you're going to replace the lost client with one who is even more valuable.
- Maintain an unequivocal trust that you will accomplish nothing less than that.
- Get back to prospecting immediately. (You'll be amazed at how much better you feel.)
- Use more aggressive strategies, perhaps ones you've considered in the past but didn't move forward on. Knock on doors, cold call, hand out coffee and business cards at the train station in the morning.
- Commit to those strategies until you have accomplished the first item above.

By setting a new goal and immediately getting to work on it, you will likely replace the lost client with one who is even more suitable and perhaps find more than one in the process, leaving disappointment behind. For me, it was the only way I knew to effectively get over the disappointment of an earlier failure.

In case you're getting the idea that I (or anyone) should take failure in stride, that's not the lesson I want to convey here. Years back, as we were growing our team, I remember observing with great interest how certain agents conducted their business. Often, it was all too obvious why some consistently met their goals and others didn't; then there were times when it wasn't so clear, particularly when two agents had similar business plans and seemed to invest a similar amount of time and resources.

But then I happened to see an interview that gave me some insight as to why some business- people consistently outperformed others. When the interviewee, basketball star Michael Jordan, was asked what separated him from the rest, the gist of what he said is that the upper echelon of players take losing personally. "It has to bother you when you lose. It has to bother you a lot."

I hadn't been expecting that response, but I thought it hit the nail on the head, and it brought to mind an agent we'd hired who had struggled to jump-start her career at another firm. She was delightful and very personable, but she wasn't getting traction with us, either, and after a period of time, she asked what I thought her biggest impediment might be to becoming a top-producing agent. I told her I thought it was important to have a competitive nature, and if she did have one, I had yet to see it. I then spoke about all the other great qualities and skills she possessed and advised her to build upon those. But after struggling to develop a customer base, she decided to leave real estate entirely.

Competition has an unusual effect on people. It often:

- Causes us to want something more intensely
- Inspires us to exert more energy and effort in attaining it
- Helps us to maintain our focus on the goal
- Infuses our creativity
- Increases our determination
- Broadens our thinking and expands possibilities
- Causes us to assess our strengths and weaknesses

I once heard another entrepreneur put it this way: "In business, if you don't have a competitive drive, people perceive you as being too nice. And then they confuse being nice with being naïve. That perception is seldom in your best interest."

What it comes down to is that if you don't win the order and it bothers you more than it does most others—and (this is key) if you channel that frustration properly—you will be inspired to improve and perfect your skills and generate more lucrative business than you ever could have imagined. The alternative is to be satisfied with the status quo, which will generally result in yet more orders being lost. So don't fear the competition—embrace it and outperform it. It's critical to the health of your business.

CHAPTER 9

TO GET DIFFERENT RESULTS, DO SOMETHING DIFFERENT

I f you haven't read *You2* by Price Pritchett, I highly recommend it. Pritchett is an internationally recognized authority on the dynamics of change, and in his book, he writes about a fly he observed while relaxing in the sitting room of an inn not far from Toronto. As he watched the fly repeatedly crash into the sitting room window as it attempted to escape to the outdoors, the insect's strategy became obvious: Try harder with raw effort and determination. But if the fly had exercised just a bit of ingenuity, if it had paused and tried other options, it might have noticed a simple solution to its dilemma: an open door across the room.

Pritchett reasoned that while this particular plan of escape, one fueled by obvious unbridled determination, made sense to the fly, it ultimately led to its death. "Trying harder isn't necessarily the solution to achieving more," Pritchett writes. "Sometimes, in fact, it's a big part of the problem. If you stake your hopes for a breakthrough on trying harder than ever, you may kill your chances for success." In other words, more of the same will likely result in more of the same.

When I began my real estate career years ago, I somehow knew that trying ever harder wasn't the way to go, though I had minimal business experience. Instead, at the start of each new year, I'd think to myself, "Al, if you would like this year to be different, if you want to continue to improve your performance, then you're going to have to do something different—something you didn't do last year."

To grow your business, leave your paradigm. Do something other realtors in your area are not doing. Think big! Or as Heraclitus wrote in 500 BC, "If you don't expect it, you will not find the unexpected, for it is hard to find...." Delivering my monthly newsletter door-to-door as previously mentioned is one such example. No one in my marketplace during the late 1980s was doing so.

Doing something different often means taking risks. Kierkegaard wrote, "To dare is to lose one's footing momentarily. To not dare is to lose oneself." I also love Picasso's words on the topic: "I am always doing that which I cannot do, in order that I may learn how to do it."

When we first launched our current operation in 2003, there was a competitor in the area whose agents weren't nearly as skilled or professional. But perception is reality, and they hustled. They also imitated an idea hatched by a local business—then marketed it as their own. They were gaining traction, and I decided I'd had enough.

I knew we had to do something different. I searched for a gap in my marketplace, a strategy used by all brilliant entrepreneurs. What does the consumer need? Often it's something they aren't even aware of. My competitive juices began to flow. Consequently, I hatched the idea for Stage-2 Home Preparation, our in-house staging company. This was well before the current rage in staging, at least in the Northeast. Our listing inventory increased dramatically, and our staged homes sold more quickly and for more money, gaining us many fans and clients, and reestablishing us as the #1 agency in our marketplace. Competition was part of it—it inspired us to act. But what sealed the deal is that we were inspired to do something different.

HOW TO GET YOUR HOME SOLD

The most frequent and significant question posed to realtors is, "What do I need to do to get my home sold?" Sticking with the tips below will accomplish that every time.

- The right time to sell depends on you. Conventional wisdom holds that the best time to sell is in spring, but my years of experience have taught me that no one season is better than another. When you're emotionally ready or there is a pressing financial need, and your home is physically ready, then that is the best time to put your home on the market.

- Don't price too high. Pricing is the most important component of successfully selling a house—and the most difficult. A good rule of thumb: If you are immediately happy with a realtor's suggested price, you are likely both aiming too high. It's not unusual for homeowners to think their home is worth more than it really is. In fact, it's unusual when they don't. Recently, we worked with a couple who believed that our firm had far and away the most expansive and effective marketing strategy. Their conundrum: They thought their home was worth more than we recommended. In fact, another agent from another firm agreed with them. Rather than simply disagreeing with the homeowners' perspective, our agent informed them that she would be better positioned to help them if she could look through the comparable sales that the other agent had used. They were happy to oblige, and we discovered that our competitor was setting the seller up for disappointment. The homeowners' property was a raised ranch, and all of the other agent's comparable sales were colonials. The problem? In Fairfield County, Connecticut, ranches tended to sell for 20% less than colonials. Yet there were no adjustments made in the agent's analysis. She left that up to my teammate. The bottom line: Analyze the relevant data in an unemotional manner, studying the realtor's comparable sales with an open mind and noting the advantages and disadvantages of each compared to your home. Ultimately, aim to price your home within 5% or less of what you and your realtor perceive to be your home's market value.

- Present your home in its best light. Buyers look for homes, not houses, and they purchase the home where they can imagine their family living and that best suits their needs. That's why staging is so essential. It's second only to pricing in terms of ensuring your home gets sold. Owners who fail to make the necessary repairs, who don't spruce up their home on the interior and exterior (including touch-up painting and landscaping) and who neglect to maintain a neat and clean appearance will chase most buyers away as quickly as realtors can find them. Once you've decluttered and made sure everything is in good repair, consider hiring a professional home-staging service. If you're interested in selling your car for the highest price, you'd wash it and have it detailed before you showed it, wouldn't you? Why not do the same for an asset that's exponentially more valuable?

- Hire a top agent. If there's anything as important as pricing and staging, it's choosing the most talented and aggressive agent, one who also has superb negotiating skills. The biggest mistake most homeowners make is hiring an agent who suggests the highest price. The second one is hiring an agent who compromises their commission. Look at their track record in getting their listings sold and at their sale price/list price ratio. A good negotiator who protects your equity will net you exponentially more than a weak negotiator who can't justify their value and compromises their own commission.

- Market creatively. The marketing strategy should include out-of-the-box thinking. That might include passing out information regarding your home at the local train station, including it on the back of a tide schedule or the schedule of a local sports team and, of course, the obvious: making a video of the home on internet platforms with high SEO. The latter should be a top priority for your agent. If the realtor's plan is not focused on networking to the entire broker community, the number of showings will suffer.
- First things first. If there is one thing I've learned in 35 years, it's that your first offer is usually your best. If the halfway point between an offer and your list price is a number you can live with, that should be your clue to negotiate.
- Know when to go lower. If you don't receive an offer after your first 10 to 15 showings, or if you don't receive showings at all, then it's time to adjust the price.
- If the showings are plentiful but you have no offers, a 5% adjustment is in order.
- If the showings are sparse, then you should adjust the price downward by 10%. Adjusting the price to a higher number, as some homeowners have the urge to do, is nonsensical.
- Keep in mind that reducing the price by X does not necessarily mean that your house is going to sell for X less. You are merely attempting to increase showings, and adjusting the price is by far the most effective way to do just that.

CHAPTER 10

SOMETIMES LOSING IS
THE WINNING MOVE

recently came across a list written by the Dalai Lama entitled "20 Ways to Get Good Karma." Number four made the greatest impression on me: "Remember that not getting what you want is sometimes a wonderful stroke of luck." Isn't that the truth? As a realtor, one of the biggest losses is when a homeowner chooses to work with someone else to sell their home, particularly when you know you provide more effective marketing and better service.

But in situations like these, or with any disappointment in life, it's imperative that you let go of the good that you lost so you can embrace the great. (Especially because the one you lost is unlikely to be as wonderful as what you imagined.)

That's exactly what I did when I established my farm area for direct mail. Not wanting to confuse the prospect since a confused prospect is a lost prospect, I marketed myself as a realtor who sold only properties in that area. That wasn't the case, of course, but I saw it as a necessary strategy in order to be perceived as that area's specialist. Although I knew I would lose business outside that area as a result, the trade-off was worth it to me. The suggestions below are meant to help you move forward after a loss.

- Ask the homeowner what they based their decision on. It's not awkward; it's good business because it can help you figure out what you need to improve upon.
- Think back on other times you got the order and reflect on how your performance differed. If the homeowner listed with someone who gave them an inflated price, take solace in knowing that you adhered to your principles. The same is true for me with personal relationships. As I once said to my oldest son, "When I think back on relationships I've had that have ended, some of which devastated me at the time, I realize upon reflection that there's no doubt it was the best thing that could have happened to me. Each left me in a better place and was inevitably followed by a much healthier situation or relationship." Your higher power knows you better than you know yourself.
- Use the time you would have allocated to servicing the client to prospecting for more business instead.

The new business you do capture may very well include a more saleable home, owned by sellers who are more in tune with your business acumen and have a greater appreciation for what you have to offer. That's how you trade good for great: by focusing on the things you can control so you can overcome the things you can't.

CHAPTER 11

CLOSE YOUR CIRCLES

I was getting ready for work, watching one of the morning shows between sips of coffee, when a guest came on who advises CEOs of some of the largest corporations in the world on organization and productivity. When asked for his best advice, he talked about neurological and physiological studies that suggest the brain is capable of fully engaging in only one task at a time. Although many claim to have the ability to multitask, the evidence simply doesn't support that notion. Multitasking doesn't work. Here are a few reasons why.

- People don't actually multitask; they switch tasks.
- It takes more time to get tasks completed if you switch between them.
- You make more errors when you switch tasks.
- Switching tasks throughout the day can cut into your productivity by 40 percent.

As a result, multi-tasking serves to:

- Negatively affect efficiency
- Compromise quality
- Increase sloppiness

Just today an agent went awry when attempting to multitask. We had a coaching call scheduled right before she was negotiating a deal. As if that wasn't enough, she had also scheduled a court time for paddle tennis earlier in the day. She did play paddle tennis but couldn't enjoy the post-match libations with her fellow players because of our appointment. Plus, since she wasn't in the office, her phone lost battery life, making her a half-hour late for our call. She would have been better off rescheduling with me ahead of time or finding another court time.

Another important piece of advice for optimizing organizational skills is to monitor your responsiveness to outside demands. One way to do that is to manage clients' expectations. It's key to set parameters for response time to client phone calls, texts and emails, for example. It's not in anyone's best interest to continually interrupt your focus by returning phone calls, texts and emails as soon as you get them throughout the entire day. Close your circles and refrain from responding to people until you've finished the task at hand. There is a book by Leo Tolstoy that has been adapted for children, entitled *The Three Questions*. These are the questions:

1. What is the right time to begin anything?
2. Who are the right people to listen to?
3. What is the most important thing to be doing at any given time?

In the book, the main character, Nikolai, in his quest to find answers, makes his way through the forest and engages in conversations with his animal friends. Eventually, he finds the answers to the first question

(Now), the second (The one you are with) and the third (Whatever you are doing in the present).

If you were to talk to my colleagues and peers, they'd say I'm someone who is well organized and maintains structure in his day. It's something I work at. When asked to explain the secret, my answer is fairly consistent. I tell others that I close my circles, meaning I try not to deviate from the task at hand until I have completed it. I work at one thing at a time.

CHAPTER 12

RECHARGE YOUR BATTERIES

On that same morning show I alluded to in the previous chapter, the organizational expert also emphasized the importance of rejuvenation and recovery. Athletes have ways to rejuvenate the body, but rejuvenating the mind is equally important. That means giving yourself some downtime to recover—something most of us don't have much of these days. The expert made a good point when he reflected that the walk back to the car after dinner or a meeting was once a time of solitude, free of work-related responsibilities. Now, with smartphones, there is no downtime whatsoever unless you create it yourself.

Creating downtime can be particularly challenging for those of us in real estate. Before we began our real estate careers, the weekend had a built-in reward: two days away from the job, two days to mentally decompress and focus on family and friends and pursue nonwork passions. Once our real estate careers began, however, the weekend evaporated before our eyes. Realtors work weekends; for most of us, it's just a way of life.

That shouldn't prevent you from putting a reward system in place. I consider it imperative, not only for the emotional benefits, but also for career longevity. I've learned to look for alternative rewards to a totally free day. When my boys were young, one reward was playing baseball with them; now, it might include tennis with a friend. Or I may drop another part of my normal routine on the weekend (like exercise) to give myself a few free and relaxing hours.

Doing this is a way of thanking the part of me that is so disciplined during the week. The breaks allow me to regenerate my creative side, which also benefits my body.

CHAPTER 13

REAL ESTATE IS
A CONTACT SPORT

Maybe some would consider me old-fashioned, but I'm a phone guy, and when I say "phone," I mean talking on the phone, not texting. There are now more ways to connect with someone than ever before. And the internet, obviously, has opened an unparalleled reservoir of possibilities for everyone, including in the real estate industry. Indeed, the origins of this book were a daily blog, as I've mentioned, and I still appreciate the chance blogging gave me to go back to my roots as an English major and combine what I've learned from my writing instructors with what I enjoy about the real estate business.

But I still prefer the cell phone to email as a means of communicating with customers or clients when possible. Here's why:

- Instant confirmation of contact (or not)
- The opportunity to connect on a more personal level

- The chance to have more in-depth dialogue
- The opportunity to learn or better respond to any questions or concerns
- The ability to clarify any misconstrued messages or false perceptions

Of course, in today's environment, it's necessary to utilize email, phone, text and social media. What you need to watch out for is using some of these methods as a "crutch" or a substitute for initiating verbal contact altogether. Some among us are fearful of rejection or confrontation and use written communication as an easier way out. This at times can elicit the opposite response you're looking for when the one you're communicating with feels more free to show their displeasure, aggression or whatever they are feeling through the written word.

I've yet to experience anything that has only an upside, including technology. It's one of life's wonderments. Anyone in this business (or any business) needs to learn how to assimilate new strategies and skills and figure out how best to use them. It's a balancing act. Take following up after open houses, for instance. An email or text to an open house visitor with links to properties that fit their parameters shows that you've listened to them and are willing to be diligent in meeting their needs. Many of us, however, sometimes use email in lieu of phoning, which is simply taking the path of least resistance.

As realtors, our days can move at such a frantic pace that it requires great skill and experience to manage it all. Developing a deeper connection is only one of a few reasons it can be more prudent to communicate verbally in addition to email or text. Another is that an email or a text message can easily be misinterpreted. Without voice inflection and the opportunity for immediate response to your client's concerns, it's too easy to jump to conclusions during anxious moments, making it harder to come up with solutions. Another drawback to email and text is that it's too inviting for the sender of the message to be less discreet and more pugnacious…even passive aggressive, to a degree. Always keep in mind that despite a client's refusal to listen to your best advice, they are nevertheless a client and should be treated as such. We are all human, but it's up to us to remain professional—the one that clients look to for support. It's during difficult discussions that you need to heed mom's advice the most: Respect the needs of others and mind your manners. To that I'd add…pick up the phone!

Sometimes, though, even the phone is not enough. Sometimes, only face-to-face will do. (I once read that it's more difficult to dislike a person, or their ideas, when you're face-to-face.) Back in the late '80s when I was just starting out, I scheduled an appointment to show condominiums to a soon-to-be-divorced man. When I met him at an open house, he told me he probably wouldn't be buying for about six months or so. It was autumn, and some of the agents in the office questioned the wisdom of attempting to service the needs of someone who wouldn't be a serious buyer until months into the new year. Personally, I didn't feel I had much to lose. I was a new agent and hadn't yet transacted much business. At the least, I might learn something, and I did: that it's difficult to judge a someone's motivation until you meet them face-to-face. So much emotion factors into a decision to purchase real estate, and those emotions are only exacerbated when a traumatic experience (such as divorce) is involved. P.S. The gentleman made an offer on a waterfront unit within the first hour of my meeting him.

There are many instances I can think of throughout the years when an agent attempted to assess a potential buyer's motivation over the phone, text or email and concluded that they weren't fully motivated, only to find that the person listed or purchased a home with another realtor who met them face-to-face. Showing up is more than half the battle. Real estate is still a "contact sport"!

CHAPTER 14

UNDER PROMISE, OVERDELIVER

Recently I had a conversation with Beverly, a representative of a company I'm doing business with. I asked her to find information about an account. After ten days, I still hadn't heard back.

When I phoned a second time, she apologized, explaining that she had been out of work for a few days and hadn't yet had time to do the necessary research. That in itself was understandable. What was frustrating is that in our first conversation, she promised to get back to me later that day.

Good service is partly based on reality and partly based on expectations. If Beverly had explained to me that it was going to take ten business days to research the information I needed, my perspective—and expectations—would have been different. I most likely wouldn't have felt the disappointment I did.

I remember one evening when I was working from home and simultaneously preparing my younger son's second meal of the evening, macaroni and cheese. At the time, he was 13 and a growing boy. As his hunger pains grew, he asked, "Dad, is it ready yet? I'm starving."

"Another ten minutes" was my immediate response. Five minutes later, I told him it was ready. "That was fast," he said with a smile as he bounced his way into the kitchen.

If I had told my son that his dinner would be ready in two minutes and it took five, his perspective would have been different. But getting the mac and cheese on the table in five minutes exceeded his expectations.

The point is clear: To become a star in the mind of your clients and the rest of the world, you want to under promise and overdeliver.

As for Beverly, she eventually called me and explained there had been an error in the account I'd phoned her about and I would be reimbursed $560. Although Beverly had broken the #1 rule of business by setting unrealistic expectations, she got herself back in my good graces by coming up with a solution that was more than satisfactory to me, reinforcing what I already knew—that most missteps in business and life can be corrected.

There's a difference, however, between under promising and overdelivering, and going above and beyond. Doing the latter can work to your detriment. I'm thinking of one winter day, after a bad snowfall, when a realtor I knew had planned a brokers' open house. When she arrived at the residence, she discovered the walkway was a sheet of ice and hazardous. So she put on her boots, found a shovel and did her best to clear a path for visitors. Or tried to. Eventually she realized the walkway actually required more chopping than shoveling.

She was not the first realtor to take on that kind of responsibility. And while you may say to yourself, "Well, there's a realtor who brought added value to her clients!" the truth is, this person confused her role with that of the property's caretaker and thus became an indentured servant. Good luck managing your client's expectations after that!

What, then, should she have done? Well, she could have called the homeowner to see if the person responsible for shoveling was available. If not, she could have canceled the open house. And if neither of those options appealed, she might have called her own snow-shoveling service, after ensuring that the homeowner would reimburse her. Not ideal, but better than taking on the responsibility for shoveling herself.

On occasion, a realtor has to scratch below the surface to determine a seller's best interest at any given moment. In the example above, the realtor's impulse to shovel is not in the seller's best interest as it blurs the line between what a realtor does and doesn't do. Moving forward, that can be detrimental to the relationship. Is the seller going to value your input as you deliver feedback, offer recommendations on price adjustments and attempt to guide them through negotiations with a buyer when, from the beginning, your role has been reduced to shoveling snow? And who is going to clean the mess the dog made before the next open house? In these cases, clients are much better served by realtors who leave the homeowners' responsibilities to them and spend their time prospecting buyers for their home.

To be clear, this is not about the realtor, or any businessperson, being disdainful of getting their hands dirty. This is about making a distinction between the added value a realtor provides and the role of someone else. Don't agree? Then don't complain when a client wants you to reduce your commission after you've shown yourself to be someone who'll shovel snow or haul wood from the backyard. You're engaging in services they could get for $25 an hour…so why would they want to pay you 6% for selling their home?

CHAPTER 15

IF YOU MAKE A MISTAKE, FIX IT

We all have lapses from time to time, when, like Beverly, we don't deliver what (or when) we promised. But keep in mind that you'll only compound the problem if you become defensive or try to justify your mistake. Instead, take this course when confronted by unhappy clients due to service that is less than stellar:

- Repeat the client's concern back to them so they know you've heard them.
- Ask if they have other concerns as well
- Assure them you will work on coming up with a solution.
- Be prompt. Be creative. Be flexible.
- Determine a resolution you can live with that will exceed their expectations.

You'll likely reaffirm their initial good feelings about you and create a customer for life.

You'll never go wrong if you make the effort to go the extra mile, especially when you've made a mistake. One time, I purchased a ceramic bowl from a company that makes stunning glassware, cutlery, handcrafted wooden and ceramic bowls and other household items. I often buy their products as wedding gifts for friends, and this time, I had the bowl personalized with my friend and his wife's name, along with the date of their wedding painted along the edge. It's a gift that always seems to be well received.

True to form, when I put in the order, the service was outstanding. But it seemed to take an eternity before I received an email asking me to approve the placement, font and size of the lettering. When I did, the subject line of the email said: "Second Request." I emailed back the corrections, then mentioned that this was in fact the "first request." Days later, after numerous emails back and forth, the final approval was given, and the bowl was eventually shipped—and appreciated by my friends.

Not long after, I received a package in the mail containing a small pair of glass candle holders with a note that read, *Thank you for your business. Best Regards, Cathy.* I thought to myself, "Now that was a nice touch!"

For those of us in service industries, it can be stressful attempting to provide perfect service, 100% of the time. In fact, that's close to impossible. Yet condemning yourself for being less than perfect is counterproductive; it impedes you from giving your client your best.

Cathy got it right. She didn't include an apology in the note, nor did she need to. But she knew there had been a number of mishaps along the way and that the most effective means of getting back in my good graces was to send me a thank-you note and a gift. The art of impeccable customer service isn't always about getting it right the first time. It's about having the professionalism and business acumen to understand how to atone for the times you don't.

WHY YOU SHOULDN'T TRY TO SELL YOUR HOME ON YOUR OWN

A qualified buyer is one who is ready, willing and able to purchase your home. Studies have shown that 85% of those who look at For Sale by Owner properties are just beginning to think about moving and have "frozen equity," meaning they are often six to nine months away from buying. They may have a home to sell before they can purchase or have credit issues that need to be remedied. These future buyers may not want to infringe upon a realtor's time until they're more serious, so they look at "By Owner" properties to get a feel for what is available, and thus aren't the "ready, willing and able" buyer you are looking for.

Another 10% of those looking at "By Owner" properties often view properties that are at a price point above what they can afford. That adds up to 95% of the "lookers," meaning most home sellers who are not using a realtor are actually working with only 5% of the high-quality buyers that exist in any given price point.

CHAPTER 16

MAKE IT PERSONAL

The personal touch never goes out of style. Every year, at our holiday party, we kick things off with gifts from Tiffany's for the support staff. There's something magical about that aqua-green box. The tradition never gets old.

One year, I received a thank-you note from the salesperson who helped me make the purchase. It read: *Dear Al, Thank you so much for your purchase of the initialed pendants and earrings. I hope to assist you again in the near future. Happy New Year! Sincerely, Rose*

The service at the store was good. The marketing and display of the jewelry was impeccable. The technology used to process my purchase was up to date. The regular emails I receive from Tiffany's are impactful. But none of these made the indelible impression that Rose's note did. I'm quite sure Rose was unaware of my annual visit to the store, but her note was an indication of what an excellent salesperson she is. She understands the power of the personal touch. There may come a day when I make a more significant purchase at Tiffany's. When I do, I'll keep an eye out for Rose, who is living the law of our universe. By thanking me for being part of her successful day, the positive energy she has shared will no doubt come back around, somehow, some way. If you add a personal touch to your interactions with clients, you will create a client for life.

The opposite is also true. Recently, I received an email that contained background information about an author I was planning to hear speak in a few days' time. The plotline of her first novel seemed interesting, and I was very much looking forward to listening to her. My plan was to buy a hardcover copy of the book after she was done speaking, as those in attendance were told that she would be available to sign all of them. I arrived a few minutes early, hoping to introduce myself, but never had a chance as she was conversing with another couple the entire time.

That evening, she read two excerpts from her book as she intermittently talked about her life experiences and how those experiences shaped her writing. After entertaining a few questions, she sat down for the book signing. A few minutes in, I began to lose my appetite for waiting in line, and it didn't take long for me to understand why: Other than the conversation she'd had with the couple when I first arrived, she never really engaged anyone in a personal way. I noticed that a number of other guests were departing along with me, and I thought, "People need to feel good about you and want to know you have a personal interest in them before they really feel comfortable buying something from you."

As I left that evening, I recalled a similar situation. I was speaking to someone I'd befriended after she and her husband purchased one of my listings. I didn't know them before the purchase, and they were working with another agent, but I was present for the showing. She flat-out told me years later that they never would have purchased the house if not for me, not only because of my knowledge of the home and area, but because

I took a personal interest in them. Part of that is likability. It can be more important in the workplace than you think, and, in fact, it trumps a lot of other traits. Feeling comfortable with something or someone goes a long way in determining the success of the business relationship.

Similarly, I often buy lunch at a particular store in town. Sure, the food is good, but the food is good at some of the other locals, too, and costs pretty much the same. The biggest difference among them is my comfort level walking in. The place I favor creates an atmosphere using the same concept we employ when we stage our homes: the space is streamlined, light, bright and clean. It even smells good, and in a psychological sense, the space itself somehow suggests that the food is fresher and healthier.

The same goes for judging people. When we've hired employees over the years, we've often been fortunate enough to find at least two candidates who seem particularly well suited. The choice tends to boil down to which candidate is going to be the easiest to work with, the most adaptable and will fit in best with our culture.

You've likely had the same experience hiring someone yourself. If I get an estimate from a painter, the painter's reputation and cost are certainly important considerations. But I will likely find at least two who are similarly priced and have impeccable testimonials. In the end, my choice will be determined by whoever I think I can work with more comfortably. Always be mindful of how you relate to others. Likability and comfort level go a long way in shaping perceptions of who might be the best fit and whose vision is most aligned with yours.

Of course, everyone has a unique style and personality. Some people are more inclined to interact with clients than others. Yet the above examples are very telling. Likability is important, and it comes from being personable. If you're likable and personable, you're sure to increase your sales exponentially.

Recently, I walked through a home with a real estate agent as a favor, to assist her in pricing. As is so often the case when you help someone out, you learn something as well. Her way of interacting with the potential client was impressively unique. She displayed an unusual combination of congeniality and professionalism, a balance that not many are able to achieve. If I had to choose one word to describe her approach, I would have to say "engaging."

After we left the home, I complimented that realtor, noting that the potential client was clearly hanging on her every word and seemed enamored of her approach. It was obvious he trusted her perspective. When I asked her to describe her mindset as she entered appointments such as that one, she said, "I keep it simple. Everyone just wants to be loved."

I thought about that, and it's so true. Love inspires sharing and breeds security, trust and confidence, traits that are especially meaningful when you are about to embark on a business relationship involving someone's most treasured possession—their home.

So what's the best way to create engagement, to make others feel heard, understood and even loved? One thing to remember is that however much transparency is involved when two people are communicating, there is always more information to be shared and uncovered. Never assume full disclosure in any situation.

I'm amazed at the things I can learn from people simply by asking questions. Communication is a process, and asking questions is the key to an intimate relationship, whether with your children or spouse or in a business endeavor. Why is this so important to understand? One reason is that the intrinsic nature of all communication is to learn about another individual's needs, desires and goals and, if they are to become clients, to try and identify how you might assist them. The best way to get them to open up is to establish a connection, whether through interest in their pets, their children, a book you see on their coffee table, a college diploma on a wall or a display that reveals a mutual passion.

Those of us who achieve success in real estate are able to do so because we understand that the more we learn about others, the more capable we are of helping them. Which is precisely what life is about.

CHAPTER 17

DON'T SELL BEYOND THE CLOSE

"Selling beyond the close" is a common blunder, one that many of us make in sales and life. The phrase refers to a scenario where someone continues to sell a service or an idea to someone after that person is already convinced of the benefits. I remember attending a presentation made by two salespeople who had already convinced the sellers to do business with them; the clients were clearly ready to end the meeting and sign the contract. But rather than move forward with getting signatures, the presenters continued to sell the benefits of doing business with them, time ran out and the homeowners had to leave. As a result, they lost the moment and eventually the business to someone else.

Selling beyond the close can:

- Suggest that the person doing the selling has lost confidence in what they are offering

- Try the patience of the one who is being sold
- Cause the potential client to doubt the credibility of the salesperson
- Impede the salesperson from identifying ideal closing opportunities
- Ultimately lose the order

Going beyond the close can be as egregious as missing a closing signal altogether. In real estate, you never know when the next opportunity may present itself. Don't let this critical error in judgment get between you and your ability to help others. Once you hear agreement from the other party on what you're selling, it's time to get signatures and move on.

CHAPTER 18

HAVE THE COURAGE
TO BE CANDID

recently found myself wondering about the various traits that make a successful business person. I came to the conclusion that courage and candor are major contributors. As Winston Churchill said, "Courage is rightly esteemed the first of human qualities...because it is the quality which guarantees all others." This was confirmed for me when I listened to yet another young author speak at our local library. She read passages from her first novel, which had been released to very positive reviews, and among other things talked about the way in which she selected the agent who helped her get the book published. It came down to the relationship. The agent she chose was the one who gave her the most guidance and was there to advise her every step of the way. As a new author, that was very important to her.

Many of our clients are new to the process of selling a home, and because of the extreme emotions often involved, it takes courage to tell them candidly what they need to know rather than what they want to hear. The candor and courage to do so is what separates the exceptional agent from those who are simply better than average. Those who are too timid to note the facts for fear of losing the business are most often not very successful. The potential client will sense their weakness and they'll likely end up losing the business anyway, or they won't demonstrate the assertiveness and acumen it takes to get the property closed.

As I sat in on the tail end of a listing presentation, I remember the homeowner turning to me and saying, excitedly, "We found the house we live in now through an ad in *The New York Times*!"

"How long ago did you say you bought it?" I politely questioned.

"Well, it's almost 40 years ago now," he replied with a smile.

"That's certainly not a surprise, then—that was long before the internet. Did you know print advertising has accounted for only 1% of buyers over the past six months?"

"Wow," he replied. "I suppose things have changed."

About 20 years ago, a non–team member asked me to share a listing she was pitching within my neighborhood of expertise. I agreed, and at the end of the presentation the homeowner reviewed the listing paperwork, wondering about the lack of specificity regarding the room dimensions of his home. The other agent quickly piped up, "Oh, we can add them—I'll do that right now."

"Let's think about this first," I challenged. "Imagine someone who is moving from across the country looking at your listing online. Do we really want them to decide that your home isn't suitable because they've calculated that your dining room won't accommodate their dining room table? Let's have them fall in love with the house first and then make that determination."

"Great idea!" the homeowner agreed.

Realtors who are at the top of their game don't tell clients or potential clients what they want to hear. Instead, they give them their best advice. In return, they gain their client's respect and help them get to the closing table more often. Anything short of that is simply enabling them to believe what they believe, whether accurate or not.

Some situations require more courage than others, especially when there are no easy solutions at hand. Business people avoid frank discussions with their clients for a variety of reasons, including:

- Fear of disturbing the relationship
- Fear of giving advice that backfires or fails
- Insecurity with their knowledge, skill set or capabilities
- It's easier to just keep quiet

The irony is that the relationship is more likely to become unsettled if you give no advice at all. The absence of advice also increases the opportunity for failure.

In business, lack of input is the equivalent of stagnation. When you stay silent, you are essentially advising someone to do nothing. In real estate, at least, we are hired to assist a client in moving forward toward their goals. If fear impedes realtors from doing that, why accept the responsibility in the first place?

It can feel easier, safer and less risky to avoid speaking up and addressing problems. But what I've found is that people with small dreams and ambitions address the small problems and avoid the large ones—and I've seldom seen them grow. They also miss out on creating a reputation for "tackling the tough ones." In real estate sales, assertiveness wins the day. Your clients need your advice, especially when they are frustrated. Tell them what they need to know to meet their goal so they can pursue their dreams.

CHAPTER 19

PAY ATTENTION TO ATTENTION SPANS

Being a good realtor means being a good communicator. Part of that is understanding how to keep someone's attention. It's not always easy. During normal, everyday activities, our mind wanders up to 30 percent of the time. Thus, the more ways you find to grab and hold someone's attention, the less your audience's mind will wander. No matter how hard we want to concentrate, humans won't always be able to focus on one thing. Indeed, study after study has shown that sustained attention lasts about ten minutes, yet most business presentations last for an hour.

To keep everyone's attention, it's essential to change your pace, visuals and points of interest at least every six minutes. Here are the best ways to keep things varied and unpredictable:

- Ask questions.
- Tell accompanying stories.

- Maintain Interaction.
- Change topics in a way that makes sense.
- Appeal to the listener's logic and reasoning, as well as their emotions and survival instincts.
- Be yourself—no one style is necessarily better than another.
- Have plenty of visuals on hand.
- Use the presentee(s) name—often.
- Smile. Even better, display a sense of humor and a "human side."
- Make eye contact.
- Engage by involving your audience in the conversation.
- Make your points in a logical, coherent sequence.
- Ask questions often.
- Really listen to the answers and show you are doing that by intermittently repeating back what your listeners say.
- Watch for nonverbal cues such as lack of eye contact, fidgeting, etc., and respond by asking listeners if they understand the benefit of what you are presenting or by moving on to your next point.
- Ask for the order by asking if they are ready to move forward with you.

Whatever your style, it's normal to get a bit nervous before presentations. Pay attention to what you're feeling. If you are very anxious, that's often an indication that you are focusing too much on the benefits to you versus the benefits to your potential client. Remember—you are there to help.

If you are a strong presenter and follow these tips, you should secure the business you are pursuing a minimum of 80% of the time. When you don't, ask yourself, "What did I do better during this presentation than the last presentation when I did secure the business?" Then proceed to build on that positive energy and mindset. It's an idea I got from one whom many consider to be the greatest golfer of all time, Tiger Woods.

When he was growing up, his father would impart those words of wisdom whenever Tiger was distraught about not winning a tournament. Although seemingly counterintuitive, it was actually great advice. I advise team members to think this way because it encourages them to think about the positive side of their performance in an effort to do better next time and improve their overall success rate.

CHAPTER 20

ADJUST YOUR DEMEANOR AND DIALOGUE TO THE CUSTOMER

I f you relate with every person (or customer) in the same way, you will lose out on many opportunities. To succeed in this world and in business, it's essential to learn to communicate effectively with all personality types. Most of us know this, yet we often forget it during real-life encounters.

When choosing a realtor, I've found that some potential clients care most about the person. They often have little interest in the way things are done—the process. They want to communicate; they need to understand what you're about and how you interact with others. They formulate an opinion based on a feeling they get from speaking with you, even if on an unconscious level. They often make decisions based on "gut instincts," including when it comes to important decisions about pricing their home and with whom to list.

Others are much more interested in the process. They don't give much thought to their general feelings when it comes to hiring someone; they are more focused on learning how to get from point A to point B, the marketing plan and strategy for finding buyers. They want all the details, and when you talk with them about pricing, you better have in-depth statistics to substantiate your recommendations. They are methodical decisionmakers and won't decide until they've had the opportunity to analyze all the facts.

Communicating with the first type, a "people person," is not so difficult if you happen to be a people person yourself—and the same goes for process people. The challenge comes when you encounter someone who is different from you. Most of us, even successful salespeople, are not both. Communicating with our opposite takes patience and is even something of an art form. Learning how to do so is an attribute that places you at the upper echelon of your craft.

Then, of course, there are people who are just plain challenging. For me, those tend to be people who are overly focused on the statistics. I'm a very "bottom line" person whose energy is focused on the results despite what the statistics indicate should be occurring. If the results are suggesting one course of action and the statistics indicate another, I'll go with the results every time. The statistics may indicate one price while the market's reaction is suggesting another, and the market's reaction is all that really matters.

To communicate with someone you find difficult (or to be your opposite) try these tips:

- Maintain self-control. When you lose that, you also lose your client's respect. Once that occurs, it's extremely difficult to get it back.
- Ask nonthreatening questions. When individuals are placed on the defensive, communication usually breaks down.
- Listen to their reasoning. They may offer a perspective you haven't thought of before.

- Acknowledge the problem—it's an effective way of showing you understand.
- Don't argue. It puts people on the defensive and creates a total breakdown in communication.
- Empathize. Verbalizing that you care lays the foundation for a solution-oriented discussion.
- Offer solutions. That's part of the value you bring.
- Continue to act professionally. It's tough to maintain a good reputation when you don't.
- Analyze what went wrong. Seek to understand things you could have done differently without dwelling on them; this can be helpful when a difficult situation arises again.
- Set limits as to what you will tolerate. Sometimes a relationship just isn't going to work. Your fiduciary responsibility to your client does not include tolerating abuse of any kind. If a client continues to display a lack of respect for you or your professionalism, it may be time to cut ties.

CHAPTER 21

MASTER THE ART OF
NEGOTIATION

N egotiating is essentially the art of influencing or persuading others. All of us have to negotiate in life, whether in business, in marriage, or with our children, and there is a lot of psychology involved. But if you understand some fundamentals, you'll find it's easier to get what you want while leaving the other party happy.

When interacting with a potential client who would like to list their home, you have to create the most favorable conditions possible, beginning with communicating directly with the decision maker(s), preferably face-to-face, as I've mentioned. Face-to-face communication reduces the risk of misunderstandings and will give you more insight into the other person's motivation or hesitations. Additionally, taking the time to meet in person with the decision maker earns the prospect's respect for your professionalism and business acumen. In short, if you're not communicating directly with the decision maker, you're not really negotiating at all.

Some other rules to live by when negotiating:

- Work within a range that includes minimums, targets and maximums…be they financial, a commodity or otherwise.
- Stay focused, calm and unflappable.
- Understand the issues and empathize, but don't let emotions distract you.
- When you make a concession, ask for something in return. (More on concessions, below.)
- When you hit an impasse, settle everything else first and then return to it.
- Remain flexible and open to a range of options.
- Always under promise and overdeliver. (I've said this before, but it's worth repeating.)

One absolutely fundamental facet of negotiating that many of us tend to forget is that negotiations are a matter of give and take. Both parties need to feel they've come away with a win; if they don't, there's no reason for them to make the deal. Similarly, the importance of making concessions, though often overlooked, is crucial to both parties walking away satisfied. It may seem strange to talk about concessions in a chapter about negotiating, but there is an art to it, as I teach in my "Master Class on Negotiations." Here are some tips to keep in mind—they are focused on real estate but apply to nearly any situation where you are trying to come to an agreement.

- Point out each concession as it is offered. Make it clear that what you are giving up has value to you.
- Emphasize the benefits of the concessions to the other side.
- Don't give up on your original demands too quickly; they just might be accepted if you maintain your determination.

The following is also imperative when concessions are on the table, as they are with every negotiation:

- Define and expect reciprocity; diplomatically insist upon it. For example, "I can totally understand how you feel. However, you're asking me to abandon a process that has, over the years, been instrumental in maximizing our clients' equity, and it would be very unprofessional of me to do that to you."
- Make contingent concessions, being clear that you are offering the concession only if the other party agrees to make a specified concession in return (e.g., the buyer removes the mortgage commitment in exchange for a more favorable closing date).
- Make concessions in installments; don't request or offer everything at once and you'll have a better chance of coming to an agreement.

GLOSSARY OF INSIDER NEGOTIATING TACTICS

What sets master negotiators apart from the rest are the subtle tactics they use to help seal the deal. A familiarity with these tactics and an understanding of the most effective counterstrategies will give you a distinct advantage in negotiating the best price for your client. Below, some of my favorites:

- Pre-Conditioning: conditions that are set before negotiations begin. ("Don't even bother bringing in an offer unless it's full price.")
- Anchoring: an attempt to establish a reference point. In sales, the initial list price is the first anchor, then the offering price becomes the new one. And so on. When negotiating, people tend to "grab" an anchor whether it's relevant or not.
- Hot Potato: one party attempts to make their problem that of their counterparts. E.g., a low offer is made because the buyer can't afford the asking price...thus attempting to make their problem that of the sellers.

- The Use of Higher Authority: bringing in the need for someone else's approval. ("We can't sign the agreement tonight because we never make a decision like this without consulting our attorney.")
- The Power of Legitimacy. One example would be making an offer supported by data that substantiates or "legitimizes" your price.
- Nibbling: when one party is continually asking for more. ("By the way, the play set in the backyard would be perfect for our children's age. Would the seller mind including that in the sale?")
- The Vice: an attempt to induce your counterpart to negotiate against themselves. An agent responds to a low offer with, "You will have to do better than that." Essentially, it's a technique to inspire the other side to negotiate against themselves.
- Splitting the Difference: an attempt to achieve a sense of fairness. When seller and buyer are X amount apart, both agree to meet in the middle.
- The Deadline: setting a time frame within which an offer will be withdrawn. ("We need an answer by 5:00 P.M., or we're moving on to another home.")
- The Withdrawn Offer: when an offer is verbally withdrawn.
- The Other Buyer: a tactic used to create fear. ("We have another buyer who is very interested.")
- Big Favor, Little Favor: requesting a large concession in hopes of receiving a smaller one that's more important to you. For example, asking for a more expensive item, such as the aforementioned play set, in addition to a smaller concession, such as a fireplace screen…which is something this particular buyer would prefer to have.
- Silence: making a proposal and remaining silent. In general, silence makes the parties in negotiations uncomfortable, and the one who speaks first generally compromises most.

*Bonus: The Flinch: a subtle sound or facial expression that communicates disappointment and plants doubts in the counterpart's mind. It's another benefit of face-to-face negotiations. When you show your counterpart a facial expression that suggests unhappiness with the situation at hand, it often speaks volumes and inspires reaction.

CHAPTER 22

HOW TO GET THE
BUSINESS YOU WANT

"The One That Got Away" is the title of a very popular song by Katy Perry, and its message clearly resounds with many. The song is about a woman who, in retrospect, regrets the end of a relationship from long ago, and my guess is that it represents a feeling many of us have experienced in various situations. In business, for instance, the one who got away is often a potential client—say, when a particular meeting goes extremely well but you don't walk away with the order. Soon after, you realize this was one you could have had.

To avoid that awful feeling, try these tips. Some may seem obvious, but they are too often overlooked.

- All meetings should be face-to-face with all decision makers.
- You should attempt to close for the business numerous times.

- If you haven't already gotten the order, have a predetermined reason to meet again.
- Push the envelope and attempt to close one more time. If they want to "think about it," ask what they will know tomorrow that they don't already know today.
- Follow up with a text or, preferably, a phone call that evening or the very next day.
- Follow up the phone call with a thank-you note that, among other things, confirms your next appointment.
- Attend your next appointment with the same exuberance you had at the start.
- Attempt to close numerous times (once again).
- If you still do not have the business when you leave, follow up, beginning with the text or phone call, all over again.

You're not going to win them all. But the ones you don't get are seldom due to being too aggressive. More often than not, it's because you weren't aggressive enough. But if your follow-up is consistent, at the very least, you'll know you did everything in your power to make it happen.

CHAPTER 23

SILENCE IS GOLDEN

We've all heard the saying "There's a reason we are blessed with two ears and one mouth." Yet many of us are uncomfortable with silence. There have been countless times in my career when I've observed a salesperson attempting to make a situation better, only to make it worse. I remember one preview showing where the listing agent offered a grandiose idea on how the entry hall could be renovated to include a huge, sweeping stairway. I hadn't noticed anything wrong with the stairway as it was. "Well, that's an interesting sales technique," I thought. "Let's encourage the buyer to spend $50K before even setting foot into a living area."

Then, at the open house, as I gazed out the glass sliding doors of the beach area property, the realtor, who was on the phone, asked whoever she was speaking with to hold. "Don't worry about the ponding in the back yard," she loudly exclaimed in my direction (from an adjoining room). "The government is attending to it and will be installing a drainage system very soon." To my mind, the beauty of the marshland was captivating; I hadn't even noticed the ponding.

"Never trust the government," I said jokingly. One man's poison is another man's pleasure.

I've forgotten the silence rule myself at times, especially early in my career. I once had a listing of a home with power lines in the backyard. Beforehand, against my instincts, I made copies of an article concluding that living near power lines was harmless. I left the copies on a table in the kitchen with other information about the home. Unfortunately, the article only served to call greater attention to the issue and exacerbate potential buyers' discomfort.

When it comes to perceived negatives, silence is golden. The worst thing you can do is to address them before you know they're a concern.

CHAPTER 24

HOLDING OUT FOR PERFECTION LEADS TO MISSED OPPORTUNITIES

D r. Joseph Ho is the Michelangelo of acupuncturists. A diminutive, gracious man, I've been seeing him intermittently for years. He's from China, where he studied medicine and where he met his wife during his 20-year confinement in a concentration camp.

Dr. Ho's office is attached to his home in the beautiful countryside of North Stamford, Connecticut. When I first began to see him, his home and office were in a much less attractive location. As he worked on me, he would often talk about his search for a new home. As a realtor who is passionate about real estate (as realtors tend to be), I couldn't help but finally comment, "Dr. Ho, you've been looking for a home for months. What seems to be the challenge?"

"It's Mrs. Ho," he sheepishly replied, referring to his wife. "Whenever we find one that I think will work well for us, she wonders if there isn't going to be another one the next day that will suit us even better." I laughed and responded, "Suggest to Mrs. Ho that if you had a similar mindset all those years ago when you proposed to her, you might both still be single!"

Dr. Ho got a charge out of that comment, and, as was his inclination whenever he heard something that amused him, he repeated it often throughout that hour session, always with a chuckle. Ultimately, he shared my comment with his wife, and at my next appointment, he informed me that they were under contract for what is now their current home.

The point: There is no perfect home, even if you have to live in one for a while before you realize that. There is also no predetermined number of homes a buyer needs to view before making an offer on one they are smitten with. Sometimes, the best opportunity is a home you view during your very first day out.

CHAPTER 25

BONUS! LIFE LESSONS FOR SUCCESSFUL BROKERS

To my mind, real estate agents address two basic human needs: security and hope. If there is anything that helps one feel secure, it's owning a home. That's what makes what we do as realtors so valuable—and why we carry such a heavy dose of responsibility.

Albert Einstein once said, "Strange is our situation here upon earth. Each of us comes for a short visit, not knowing why, yet sometimes seeming to a divine purpose. From the standpoint of daily life, however, there is one thing that we do know. That man is here for the sake of other men."

Isn't that really what our work is about—something we do for the sake of others? Think about it: Outside of the health professions and education, it would be difficult to find a vocation that impacts the lives of others as much as that of a realtor. And if we are going to make the most of our "short visit," we must affect the lives of as many people as we can. Whether you're finding a client a home or selling theirs, the deepest footprint you can make on this earth is to accomplish that in the spirit of love. The musings in this chapter, gleaned from 35 years in the field, are tailored to the real estate business, but I predict that many will give you an edge whatever business you happen to be in.

AUTHENTICITY IS KEY

There's one thing that engenders peace of mind more than anything else, and that's knowing you've remained authentic throughout your experience. Yet one of life's great mysteries is why we so often find it difficult to follow our instincts and be authentic. The truth is, if we weren't so concerned about the peripheral distractions that seem to make their way into every transaction, we would be able to allay our clients' fears more consistently—and make the sale. Luckily, the secret to providing your clients with what they need isn't as mysterious as you might think. Essentially, you need to:

- Know what a client's goals are.
- Have a plan and implement it.
- Don't allow yourself to get distracted.
- Refuse to get involved with the drama of the day.
- Don't allow yourself to be defined by the comments of others.
- Guide your clients with your best advice, based on what they need to hear, not on what they want to hear.

GET INTO THE SERVICE MINDSET

When I'm coaching a realtor-in-training who is reluctant to reach out to contacts to encourage them to sell their home or buy one, I often hear: "I feel as if I'm bothering them." But when you worry you are bothering someone, you are allowing guilt to rent space in your mind. This guilt can be paralyzing. To get rid of it, it's important to change your mindset.

First, prospecting is not about pestering. The essence of prospecting is the service a realtor can provide to someone, even before they become a client. Realtors are a font of information about the real estate market, including translating that information so it makes sense. They are also well versed in the process of buying and selling a home. By disseminating that information, we offer an invaluable service. Here are some areas of expertise you can offer:

- The tax implications when buying or selling
- Helping clients manage expectations when selling a home on their own
- Commission advice
- In-depth analysis of market conditions
- Future downsizing opportunities
- Staging services
- Relocating
- Renting
- Choosing a realtor
- The most common mistakes when buying or selling

Realizing you are in real estate to provide a service and change people's lives can help you shift your mindset and focus on what you need to do to bring your value to as many people as possible.

Keeping that top of mind, here are some crucial things you need to do to succeed:

- Prospect, prospect, prospect. All of your knowledge, intelligence, skill, congeniality and care are meaningless if the people who are buying and selling homes don't know who you are. You must prospect and market consistently to be a successful realtor.

- Build rapport. That means making prospective and current clients feel that you listen and that their goals are your priority.
- Discover a client's needs. It's difficult to help your client reach their goals if you don't understand what they are looking for and need.
- Offer solutions. If your prospects perceive you to be solution oriented, they will be your client for life.
- Get to a decision. Successful realtors are very skilled at leading someone to a "yes" or "no" instead of a "maybe"—that decisiveness is almost always in everyone's best interest.

MOTIVATION MATTERS

Whatever your skill level, there are certain truisms that realtors need to understand to build a successful business. I am not being hyperbolic when I write that you violate the tenets below at your own risk:

- When meeting with current or potential clients, spend more time learning their motivation than anything else. Having an accurate understanding of what it will take to help them achieve their goals, and offering solutions to get them there, means less pain for everyone.
- You work for free until closing, so work with those who are highly motivated to close quickly.
- Be a leader. Generating seller leads is the only way to shine.
- Those who list last….
- Know the difference between good and great. Many agents do well in great markets; great agents do well in challenging markets.
- Maintain marital harmony. Refrain from writing offers on a property until both partners have seen it.
- Never the twain shall meet. A face-to-face meeting between buyer and seller before closing is seldom a good idea.

- Always say NEVER. Allowing buyers to occupy a home prior to closing is a mistake you'll make only once.
- Be a closing pro. Clients remember the closing experience as much as they remember the price.

FIRST IMPRESSIONS ARE CRUCIAL

Whether you realize it or not, potential clients are often sizing realtors up when they call about a specific property. Your knowledge of inventory, your ability to engage and, most of all, your enthusiasm will go a long way toward determining whether a caller will end up working exclusively with you. That's why the way you respond to phone calls, emails and texts is so important. If you keep these five tips in mind, you'll reap the benefits of unforeseen opportunities:

- Always introduce yourself. It seems obvious, but I'm amazed at how often the agent answering the phone recites the name of the company rather than their own name.
- Relax and speak conversationally. One of the most impressive realtors I've ever worked with answered the phone and nonchalantly engaged in conversation as if she'd known the person forever.
- Ask for the name of the caller. That same realtor, upon introducing herself, immediately secured the name and contact information of the caller.
- Be versatile. If the property a potential buyer calls about is not appropriate for them, know the inventory well enough to direct them to one that is.
- Learn Houdini's lesson. The great Houdini performed to very small crowds until he learned the art of suspense and blew up. Similarly, a caller can't comprehend all that you provide simply by hearing you over the phone. Tease them with your expertise, then make an appointment to meet with them in person.

VALUE YOURSELF

Valuing the service you provide and your special talent means not compromising your commission. That's not stubbornness or greed; a lower commission negatively affects the selling price of a client's home because an agent who doesn't value their unique talent can't possibly bring their best to others. Some agents struggle with delivering this message. When you are asked to reduce your commission, you have two basic options: 1) prove your value, or 2) cut and match. If you cut and match, you're essentially saying that you're no better than the rest, that all realtors have the same skill set. If that's the way you feel, I suggest you do what you can to improve your craft and negotiating skill set. I remember one eye-to-eye standoff on commission where, after rising from the conference room table to end the meeting and wish the home-owner good luck, we received a call literally a few minutes later from the client, who asked us to sit back down and agreed to our fee.

Potential clients want to work with someone who is assertive and confident. When you refuse to lower your standards and demonstrate that you're willing to walk away from their business, nine times out of ten, they'll decide they want your services. Get it in writing—all of it!

To serve clients to the best of your ability, it's imperative that certain events and discussions between two or more agents and their clients be noted in writing. This is especially true when negotiating offers. Below is a list of common issues, events and circumstances that should be documented:

- All offers. You might think that goes without saying, but there are areas throughout the country where offers to purchase property are made verbally.
- All terms, including price, inspection date, contract date, mortgage amount, contingency date (if there is a mortgage), and closing date. Record these as specifically as possible.
- Counteroffers exchanged between the buyer and seller.

- Any accepted backup offers. Again, the terms should be specific, and it should be made absolutely clear that these offers will go into effect only if the first agreement terminates. This sounds obvious, yet there have been occasions when, due to a lack of clarity, the sellers essentially agreed to sell their property to more than one party.
- Any issues from a building inspection.
- If the first agreement actually terminates before the contract date, the buyer's desire to withdraw their offer must be in writing. As a listing agent, you must protect your seller client in these instances. One of the last things you want is the first buyer to reappear, saying they really do want the house after all, when you have already moved on to a second buyer.
- Once the buyer's desire to terminate an agreement (after offer and acceptance but before contracts) is in writing, there is another thing to consider: In many parts of the country, a 1% down payment must accompany the initial offer; this money is held in an escrow account. Often, getting written consent from the buyer's and seller's attorneys to release those funds is required by law. Failure to get the consent in writing can put you in an unenviable position. By not following protocol, you as the agent can be liable for the 1%.

DEALING WITH DISAPPOINTING OFFERS

As Kenny Rogers sings in his famous hit "The Gambler," "You got to know when to hold 'em, know when to fold 'em." It's not always an easy decision, but the market speaks loudly and clearly. Still, some sellers, as you have likely discovered if you have even a modicum of experience, have a distorted view on the proper course of action when an offer is disappointing. Many think they should hold fast to their list price and consider only a minimal counteroffer, if any at all.

In reality, the rules are not so hard and fast. The seller's response should depend on a number of considerations. Among them:

- How long the home has been on the market. This is a reflection of the accuracy of the list price and an indication of how much leverage you have.
- How far off the buyer's offer is from the seller's bottom line
- The seller's plan B if they don't get their price

As the listing agent, it's your responsibility to help the seller remove the emotion from their decision. One of the most effective ways to do that is to focus on the third bullet point above. Ask them about their Plan B explicitly: What will you do if you choose not to negotiate with the buyer at hand and the buyer moves on?

The seller's decision not to negotiate, not to sell and to remove their house from the market may make sense—if they are prepared to remain in their home for as long as it takes for home values to improve. The listing agent needs to discover if the seller is in fact truly determined to follow through with that option or if they are merely displaying "sour grapes." Are they willing to wait until later in the year or early next year...or even five years? Are they thinking they'll simply wait until they get a better offer?

This is where your skill as a realtor comes into play. Your fiduciary responsibility is to help your client understand that they are making decisions based on things that may never happen. A subsequent offer could be at a price that, while higher, is not enough to offset the additional carrying costs accrued while the home remains on the market (mortgage, utilities, taxes, etc.). To give your clients a thorough understanding of the possibilities and guide them toward the most prudent decision, you must assist in giving them a clear vision of those possibilities. To do that, you need to establish trust by making it all about the client. Your advice to them should be the same advice you would follow if you were selling your own home. After all, it's their investment and their future, not yours, and you must always keep that top of mind.

Getting the Power Dynamics Right

One of the biggest challenges for a real estate agent is to establish a healthy balance of control with their seller clients. A home seller is entrusting their agent with a huge investment and is looking for a huge investment of time and resources in return.

A foundation of the relationship, as I mention above, is helping the seller feel a sense of security. Establish that at the beginning of the relationship and, because they trust you, the seller will generally be more open to understanding and accepting the factors that contribute to a home not selling. If that trust and security isn't established, they may have unrealistic expectations, and the focus of their disappointment will be...you.

I advise realtors to always establish the right power balance at the outset of the relationship, preferably at the listing presentation. But you must be careful: Appear too demanding and you will turn clients off before you are hired. Acquiesce to their every desire and you'll appear weak—and then good luck securing their business. To achieve the best balance, keep these tips in mind from the get-go:

- Always have the client's best interest in mind.
- Share your honest opinion, even if it's not what they want to hear. Agreeing to terms that do not work within the scope of your business model, or to a marketing plan that they request but you do not believe in, is not in their best interest and is a sure way to lose control and meet with an unsatisfying result.
- Maintain your principles when it comes to pricing.
- To best manage expectations, keep promises to a bare minimum in terms of predicting the future of the market. Ask your clients how they prefer to be communicated with, then give them specifics as to when and how often you will do that.

ESTABLISHING A HEALTHY
HOME-SELLING MINDSET

As a realtor, you're not just a businessperson; you're also a coach, and you need to provide clients with the clarity and inspiration to guide them to the closing table. I can't say it too many times: This doesn't mean telling the seller what they want to hear, but telling them what they need to know, including establishing realistic expectations. Below are some useful suggestions to help your home seller client know what to expect:

- Take the long view: When a home isn't moving, and was purchased years earlier, sellers should consider factors other than simply what they believe it's worth. Determining how much equity they've created can be helpful in that regard.
- Price to sell. If the seller has to move, no ifs, ands or buts about it, suggest they cut the price below the competition at least by their carrying costs (include mortgage payments, taxes, insurance, etc.).
- Use the rule of ten. Ten potential buyers through a client's home with no offers suggests a 5% reduction in price. If they're getting showings but no offers, that means buyers think the home is overpriced. No showings suggests the same. If that occurs, the adjustment needs to be at least 10%.
- Keep market time in mind. Buyers worry when they see a long market time; they're apt to think something is wrong with a house that doesn't sell. This, in turn, conjures up concerns about the price, or what we refer to as "incurables"—impediments that most buyers object to but that the homeowner cannot change. A major thoroughfare just beyond the property or high-tension wires and a tower nearby are obvious examples. The savvy homeowner understands that the only way to overcome these is with price.

- Let them see for themselves. Sellers might want to visit the open houses of their competition, noting the advantages of other homes compared to theirs and adjusting the price to be competitive with all of them.
- Know the value of new construction. Buyers pay a premium for new construction—up to 15% to 20% more. Your client's home should be priced lower than comparable newly constructed homes or buyers will likely purchase them instead.
- Timing. It shouldn't be determined by the season but by other factors in your client's life. The best home-selling experiences usually occur when clients are emotionally prepared and their home is physically prepared.
- Perspective is all. Remind clients that it's in their best interest to consider things from the buyer's perspective rather than becoming offended by offers that fail to meet their expectations. A small counteroffer is better than no counteroffer at all.
- The power of now. Based on current market conditions, have sellers ask themselves what they would pay for their house today given recent sales in their area, being as objective as they can.
- Consider the competition. Is the inventory in your town high? What about your price point? These are signs you need to break away from the pack and stand out (more on that below). A sharp price cut is the best way to do that.

WHY A REALTOR IS A BIT LIKE A THERAPIST, OR THE "COLD FEET" SYNDROME

You may have gone into this business thinking you would be dealing with real estate, but what you are really dealing with is emotions. And it is your job to help clients keep their emotions in check in any market. As most realtors know, the true job of selling a home begins once the contract is signed. That's where the emotional component kicks in, and when the skill of the realtor comes into play in balancing the emotions of all parties involved.

Take home inspections. There can be a huge emotional impact on the psyche of the buyer on inspection day. It's at this juncture that the buyer realizes, "Wow, I am actually buying this house. When the inspection is over and I sign formal contracts, I own this house for better or for worse."

That's when buyers can become unreasonable about seemingly minor issues. Realtors, beware: What this usually means is that they are becoming fearful of the purchase and are looking for a reason to say no. At this point you need to:

- Probe with questions.
- Help them verbalize their fears.
- Quickly give them a reason to say yes.

The thought of really and truly owning a home can be overwhelming to buyers and can often inspire irrational thoughts and behavior. This is when the buyer needs the support of their realtor more than ever, and when the right skill set can move the buyer and seller to a meeting of the minds. To make this happen, the skilled realtor:

- Engages in consistent communication with their client and the other realtor
- Maintains copious notes of every conversation with all parties involved
- Does their best to ensure emotions are kept in check
- Always negotiates for their client, not for themselves
- Always gives their client their best advice, but never makes decisions for their client
- Reminds both parties of the reasons they consummated the deal in the first place

- Helps their client and the other realtor prioritize the most important issues and avoid fixating on minor issues
- Offers a solution where both buyer and seller feel as if they have come away with a "win"

Along with the rest of the advice in this section, these are the key ingredients to providing exceptional value to your clients as well as holding together a higher percentage of your contracted properties than other realtors in your marketplace. Helping more people achieve their dreams…what could be more satisfying than that?

A FINAL WORD ON EXECUTING A SUCCESSFUL LISTING EXPERIENCE

When it comes to protecting your client's equity and procuring the highest price, you can fly banners in the sky about the offering, but if the listing is not positioned properly with respect to price, it will either sell at a significant discount or not at all. The top realtors are more persistent at helping the homeowner understand this. There are two sets of circumstances, however, where even some of the most successful realtors go wrong.

The first is treating friends differently with respect to doing business. A realtor on my team learned this the hard way. Rather than having a meeting with the friend and potential client in a thorough manner as all team members are mentored to do, she took a much more casual approach in terms of presenting our marketing plan and the most prudent price with which to enter the marketplace. Because she did not properly explain the reasoning for our suggested price, nor educate the homeowner on the value we provide, the friend ended up listing her home with someone else. The agent realized she took a much too casual approach to securing the business and told me as much. When I asked her if she heard the many times I advised on the subject of doing business with friends during our training sessions, she responded, "Yes, but I didn't believe you. I believe you now." If you treat friends differently than other clients, you will experience pain.

The second mistake occurs with high-net-worth home sellers. Many agents are so excited about listing a property at the high end of the market that they compromise their values. That's not in anyone's best interest. Moreover, they treat the owner of a high-valued property with a certain deference that in actuality is not warranted. We have had many, many clients across the socio-economic spectrum, including MBAs from the best schools in America and the most successful Wall Street tycoons. What I have come to realize is that despite a seller's economic brilliance, they are no less emotional, no more rational and usually no more accurate in their perceived value of their property than a seller who struggled to graduate from high school. Until a realtor understands this, procuring the highest price for a client will be much more challenging.

EVEN MORE ON HOW TO STAND OUT FROM THE PACK

Realtors will fall short if they don't talk to their clients about what I call "pricing ahead of the curve." To understand the way the pricing ladder works, let's use an example of a homeowner who wants to price their home at $1.550M despite your $1.425M recommendation. Let's say the seller is adamant that's it's fair to price their home "in the middle of the pack" with the competition, and the home is entered on the Multiple Listing Service at $1.550M. Now let's see how it initially compares with the competition:

- Competitive #1: $1.625M
- Competitive #2: $1.595M
- Competitive #3: $1.550M

- Subject Property: $1.550M
- Competitive #4: $1.495M
- Competitive #5: $1.475M
- Competitive #6: $1.450M

As you can see, the homeowner essentially chose to price their home in the middle of the pack.

Now, let's look at what can happen in as little as 30 days:

- Competitive #1: Withdrawn from market
- Competitive #2: Reduced to $1.499M
- Competitive #3: Reduced to $1.479M
- Subject Property: Price remains at $1.550M
- Competitive #4: Price remains at $1.495M
- Competitive #5: Under Contract
- Competitive #6: Under Contract

Additionally, two more comparable homes have come on the market listed at $1.475M and $1.450M.

Now let's see how the subject property stacks up compared to the repositioned competition.

- Subject Property: $1.550M
- Competitive #1: $1.499M
- Competitive #2: $1.495M
- Competitive #3: $1.479M
- Competitive #4: $1.475M
- Competitive #5: $1.450M

By initially pricing their home in the middle of the pack, the home-owners have now set themselves up to become the most expensive listing of all the comparable homes. The end result is a longer market time, which generally means the home will sell for less. That's why it makes sense to price your home "ahead of the curve," so it stands out from the competition.

Yet at times, all the competitive and comparable properties in the world will not be enough to convince a homeowner of the proper price. In these cases, I have found that including a visual graphic or two in your arsenal can help them see the light. One I particularly like is from real estate educator David Knox:

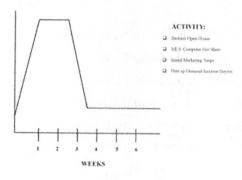

ACTIVITY:
- ❏ Broken Open House
- ❏ MLS Computer Hot Sheet
- ❏ Initial Marketing Surge
- ❏ Pent up Demand Anxious Buyers

WEEKS

Over pricing your home when the best customers come through and lowering it after they're gone.

If you're an experienced realtor, you've no doubt heard a homeowner proclaim, "Well, we can't go up, but we can always come down." This may be true in theory, but the above graphic shows the downside to such an approach. Realtors know that the best buyers tend to view the home when it first comes on the market. In contrast, less motivated buyers, those with frozen equity, or those who are looking for a deal or are thinking of buying "sometime down the road" tend to come through once a property has lingered on the market. The consequences may include the home languishing on the market for months, a price adjustment that is even lower than where it initially should have been priced and the property selling for less than it would have if priced properly from the beginning.

Lesson learned (I hope). The next time a homeowner asks, "Shouldn't we just try it at a higher price?" you now have enough evidence to reply, "Well, actually, we shouldn't…and here's why."

CPSIA information can be obtained
at www.ICGtesting.com
Printed in the USA
BVHW041526171222
654415BV00002B/299